# Professional Foc
# Managen

C000200842

This is a handbook for leading a professional football club to commercial success. Covering every aspect of the business and commercial operations of a modern football club, and with a focus on increasing revenues and building a powerful brand, this book explains how to take any club to the next level and increase brand value.

Drawing on the author's extensive experience of working in elite professional football, this book covers all the core areas of club management, from brand identity, brand positioning, strategy and planning, human resource management and developing partnerships, to marketing, ticketing, venue operations and merchandise. It examines the importance of business models and achieving club stability and sustainability, and introduces cutting-edge topics that are having an increasing impact on the development of football clubs, including corporate social responsibility, eSports and women's football. This book is full of real-world cases and data, and offers clear theoretical and practical guidance in every chapter.

This book is essential reading for anybody working in professional football and for anybody taking courses in executive football education, football studies or sport management. It is also a valuable resource for anyone who has a general interest in the business and commercial aspects of managing a professional football club.

**Simon Van Kerckhoven** is Founder of the football business consultancy firm, DIAS – Developing Intelligence and Advice in Soccer, located in Belgium. He was previously Chief Operating Officer of the Belgian football club Lommel SK and a consultant for City Football Group. In addition, Simon has advised multiple investors on the acquisition of football clubs and football business strategies. Recently, Simon founded Zurafa Football Capital, a private equity fund focused on investments in high-potential, undervalued football clubs.

# Professional Football Club Management

## Leadership for Commercial Success

Simon Van Kerckhoven

Routledge
Taylor & Francis Group

LONDON AND NEW YORK

Designed cover image: Paul Rushton / Alamy Stock Photo, Pixabay / www.pexels.com and Katrien Grevendonck

First published 2024
by Routledge
4 Park Square, Milton Park, Abingdon, Oxon OX14 4RN

and by Routledge
605 Third Avenue, New York, NY 10158

*Routledge is an imprint of the Taylor & Francis Group, an informa business*

*British Library Cataloguing-in-Publication Data*
A catalogue record for this book is available from the British Library

ISBN: 978-1-032-32065-6 (hbk)
ISBN: 978-1-032-32064-9 (pbk)
ISBN: 978-1-003-31268-0 (ebk)

DOI: 10.4324/9781003312680

Typeset in Optima
by codeMantra

# Contents

Contents

# Preface

With great pleasure, I present this handbook on professional football club management and the role of leadership in pushing a club toward commercial success. My passion for football and my career in the industry have brought me to this point, and I am grateful for the opportunity to share my experiences and knowledge with others.

My journey in the football world began during my studies in Sports Management, where I knew that I wanted to pursue a career in the football business. During this time, I met Jos Verschueren, the Director of Sports Management at the University of Brussels – VUB. Our shared passion for the sport and similar views on the challenges facing the football industry led us to collaborate on the launch of the International Postgraduate Course in Football Business at the University of Brussels, coordinated by the International Football Business Institute (IFBI), a football business consultancy company we co-founded.

As a co-founder at IFBI, I gained a unique perspective on modern football club management through my daily conversations with experts in the industry. The challenges and complexities I encountered in this role inspired me to write this book and share my ideas with others.

In 2020, I sold my shares at IFBI and became a consultant for City Football Group, where I brokered the acquisition of Belgian football club Lommel SK. My appointment as the Chief Operations Officer at Lommel SK provided valuable practical experiences in the football industry and reinforced my desire to share my knowledge through this book.

This handbook combines my professional activities with writing and encompasses a theoretical and practical approach, drawing on my experiences, knowledge, research, and expertise. I am grateful for all the guest lectures at IFBI and the insightful conversations I had with experts such as, among others, Don Dransfield, Olivier Jarosz, Richard Lamb, Karl Dhont, Benjamin Steen, Claudio Borges, Stijn Francis, Daniel Geey, Paolo Monguzzi, Georg Pangl, Nick Speakman, Peter Willems, Tom Rowell, Matthijs Withagen, Mathieu Moreuil, Vincenzo Ampolo, Giorgos Lagaris, Bas Schnater, Geoff Wilson, and Thomasz Zahorski.

I want to thank my former business partner Jos Verschueren for his guidance in my career and my former colleague and co-author, Martijn Ernest, who contributed to several chapters of this book. Last but not least, I would like to thank Simon Whitmore, Rebecca Connor and the entire Taylor & Francis Group for their guidance, trust and help in the development of this book.

This book is intended for those who seek a better understanding of the commercial side of professional football clubs and for industry professionals who aim to develop growth strategies or perform an audit of their club's current commercial operations.

# Disclaimer

This book represents the author's opinion and does not reflect the official point of view of the organisations for which the author works or worked. Nor do any of the statements suggest affiliation with the organisation's way of working by which the author is professionally contracted. It must be clear that all views expressed in this book belong to the content creator and not the organisations (its affiliates or employees) to which the author can be professionally linked.

# Contributor biography

**Martijn Ernest** is Account Manager Sports, Music & Events at AB InBev and former Partnerships Sales Manager at Belgian football club, Royal Sporting Club Anderlecht. He previously worked as a Business Development and Research Specialist at IFBI – International Football Business Institute.

PART

I

# General framework of football club management

# 1 Introduction to football business

Fan protest has existed since the early years of football but has become more prominent and memorable in recent years. Famously, supporters of Manchester United FC have been protesting since 2005 against the Glazer family, who set the club for sale in 2022. The fans of Borussia Dortmund once protested by throwing tennis balls on the pitch, demanding cheaper ticket prices in the German Cup games, as did the fans of Liverpool FC against the price increase of the tickets after the new stand was opened. Not so long ago, Arsenal FC fans protested outside the Emirates Stadium against the owner Stan Kroenke. However, the situation became calm again since their excellent 2022–2023 season.

Often these protests result from bad sporting results and not achieving goals on the pitch. Sometimes, like in the case of Borussia Dortmund and Liverpool, the protest has been against certain decisions that the management team has taken. Football club leaders – managers – have the challenging task of competing on the pitch and living up to the expectations of the fans and other stakeholders. Off the pitch, many clubs struggle with the connection and a deeper understanding with fans. Fans want to feel that football club leaders are listening and involving them in deciding matters that affect fans the most.

Football has changed drastically in recent decades. Sporting results go hand in hand with revenues and commercial growth. Clubs compete with each other by taking bigger financial risks yearly, leading to an increase in wages and transfer fees. Due to growing commercial interests, the game is affected by new financial flows. In August 2017, Paris Saint-Germain shattered the erstwhile transfer record by paying 222 million euros for the Brazilian superstar Neymar. Next, over the season 2017/2018, the Premier

DOI: 10.4324/9781003312680-2

League saw a transfer expenditure record of £2.4 billion, a substantial increase of 47% (Deloitte, 2019).

Aside from investing in players, incredible resources have been allocated to build new stadiums. The Mercedes-Benz Stadium, home ground of MLS club Atlanta United FC and shared with NFL team Atlanta Falcons, had a total construction cost exceeding 1.3 billion euro, making it football's most expensive venue worldwide (Rollins, 2019).

The changes in the business model of professional football can be seen across borders and balance sheets. For example, the investments in stadiums across Hungary, where ten completely new stadiums have been built since 2014. Or in Belgium, where Belgian clubs have spent 141 million euros on player transfers in the 2019 summer transfer window. The relatively small league of Denmark is another clear example of the change that has occurred: in one year, there has been an average increase of 8% in players wages (UEFA, 2018a). The reason why clubs have been spending more in recent years is to be found in the optimisation of revenues.

COVID-19 had a significant impact on club revenues. In the summer of 2020, when the virus was already globally spread, most countries were in lockdown, and some countries had already decided that there would not be any fans in the stadium that season. CIES Football Observatory stated in a report that the transfer spending from the clubs in the top five leagues in the summer of 2020 was 43% less than the record year in 2019. During that transfer period, we also saw an increase of approximately 7% in loans and free-agent transfers – (no transfer fees were paid for players). As the pandemic continued to have a big impact in the 2021–2022 season, some football clubs saw a considerable drop in revenue. In the Deloitte Football Money League report, the average revenue of the 20 Money League clubs was €409m in 2020/2021, which was a 12% decrease on the 2018/2019 season due to the absence of fans on match days. Deloitte confirms in its report that the 20 Money League clubs combined have missed out on well over €2 billion of revenue over the 2019/2020 and 2020/2021 seasons due to COVID-19. However, not all financial difficulties that some clubs face result from COVID-19.

How well are football clubs managed? If they achieve incredible sporting results and revenues keep rising yearly, then there is no reason for change, right? Unfortunately, on the other side of the football spectrum, many football clubs have huge debts, including small and big ones. FC Barcelona had in August 2022 a reported total debt of €1.35 billion! (The Athletic, 2022). Nevertheless, they were still buying expensive players for a total exceeding €150 million in the summer transfer window in 2022 (Transfermarkt, 2022). The future will tell if it was smart to sell their broadcasting and commercial revenue rights and spend most of it on player transfers.

In the UEFA Club Licensing Benchmarking Report for the financial year 2018, the top 20 clubs with the highest net debt are listed, with Manchester United FC leading the table with a net debt of €568m in 2018 and a yearly debt growth of 24%. Could this be one of the reasons for the fan protests? Within this list of 20 clubs, six of them are English clubs (Manchester United FC, Tottenham Hotspur FC, Brighton & Hove Albion FC, Watford FC, Liverpool FC, and Everton FC), four clubs are from Italy (Internazionale FC, AC Milan, Juventus, and AS Roma) and three are from Turkey (Fenerbahçe, Galatasaray AS, and Besiktas JK). However, it is important to look at net debt in context as the debt taken on to finance investments, such as Tottenham Hotspur FC did with the construction of their new stadium, is far less risky compared to the debt taken on to fund operating activities, which can lead to financial sustainability issues for those clubs. While clubs like AC Milan, Liverpool FC, Galatasaray AS, and Atlético de Madrid are decreasing their net debt year-on-year, a bigger issue arises for Fenerbahçe, with a 1.2 multiplier of net debt over long-term assets. FC Barcelona is not included in this list, as these numbers are from the 2018 financial year (Table 1.1).

To put these numbers into perspective, we need to look at the life cycle of football clubs and their continuous hunger for success. What is driving them to keep investing in players? It all starts with the institutional logic of football, the aim, and ambition for sporting success.

## Key takeaways

- Not every football club is managed in a good and sustainable way.
- Fans can have a big influence on the club and its management.
- Sporting success does not always mean that the club is successful, nor does it mean that a club is mismanaged if sporting results are not meeting expectations.
- Revenues keep growing yearly but so do wages and transfer fees.

*Table 1.1* Top 20 football clubs with highest net debt in 2018

| Rank | Club | FY18 net debt (m) | Year-on-year growth (%) | As multiple of revenue | As multiple of long-term assets |
|---|---|---|---|---|---|
| 1 | Manchester United FC | €568 | 24 | 0.9× | 0.2× |
| 2 | Tottenham Hotspur FC | €483 | 2,762 | 1.1× | 0.3× |
| 3 | FC Internazio-nale Milano | €461 | 5 | 1.6× | 0.5× |
| 4 | Club Atlético de Madrid | €384 | −8 | 1.1× | 0.4× |
| 5 | Juventus | €372 | 29 | 0.9× | 0.5× |
| 6 | Fenerbahçe SK | €334 | 49 | 2.9× | 1.2× |
| 7 | AS Roma | €312 | 42 | 1.3× | 0.7× |
| 8 | Valencia CF | €274 | 29 | 2.6× | 0.5× |
| 9 | AC Milan | €260 | −4 | 1.2× | 0.6× |
| 10 | Brighton & Hove Albion FC | €260 | n/a | 1.6× | 0.9× |
| 11 | PFC CSKA Moskva | €238 | 4 | 2.8× | 0.6× |
| 12 | FC Porto | €214 | 21 | 2.0× | 0.5× |
| 13 | VfL Wolfsburg | €196 | 96 | 1.0× | 0.7× |
| 14 | LOSC Lille | €186 | 133 | 3.5× | 0.9× |
| 15 | Besiktas JK | €183 | 3 | 1.1× | 0.9× |
| 16 | Watford FC | €177 | 76 | 1.2× | 0.8× |
| 17 | Galatasaray AS | €175 | −29 | 1.5× | 0.8× |
| 18 | Olympique Lyonnais | €173 | 0 | 1.1× | 0.3× |
| 19 | Liverpool FC | €160 | −29 | 0.3× | 0.2× |
| 20 | Everton FC | €152 | n/m* | 0.7× | 0.4× |

*Everton FC posted a positive net cash position in FY2017, so the year-on-year growth rate is not meaningful in this case. (Courtesy of UEFA, 2018b.)

# References

The Athletic. (2022). *Barcelona Money Financial Crisis*.

Deloitte. (2019). *AroFF*. p. 28.

Rollins. (2019). *SI*. para 1.

Transfermarkt. (2022). *FC Barcelona Season 22/23*. Retrieved from Transfermarkt.be.

UEFA. (2018a). *Club Licensing Benchmarking Report Financial Year 2018*.

UEFA. (2018b). *The European Club Footballing Landscape*. https://www.uefa.com/ MultimediaFiles/Download/OfficialDocument/uefaorg/Clublicensing/02/64/06/ 95/2640695_DOWNLOAD.pdf

# 2 | The continuous circle of football clubs

Many football clubs have existed for decades, some even for a century. However, the best football clubs in the world we know today have not always been the best. Multiple football clubs have disappeared due to bankruptcy or unsustainable management. Football clubs have an important role in the community. Therefore, the Continuous Circle is an important model explaining the simplicity and complexity of growing a football club to the top. Nevertheless, there are different ways to look at this model, hereunder is explained how most football club owners look at it and what is a more sustainable way to comprehend the model (Figure 2.1).

A football club starts investing in players or 'increases investments in the team'. From there, sporting success will follow as the club invests in better players. Through sporting success, brand awareness will automatically increase, which will result in recruiting more fans. A bigger fan base means, without a doubt, an increase in stadium attendance and digital audience (social media followers), which is important to attract new and higher-quality sponsors. These combined factors will result in more revenues for the club to reinvest in improving the team by buying new players. It sounds like an easy road towards winning the Champions League, right? But is this model as good and beautiful as often suggested or implemented by owners?

Buying new players often involves huge transfer fees and increased costs such as wages, housing, and cars. Football club owners usually aim to achieve the best sporting results in the shortest possible time. A football club faces short-term risks due to the high expenditure, and often, there is no long-term plan. Football clubs often focus on the next season from a strategy point of view, in the best case, but often that focus is limited to the

DOI: 10.4324/9781003312680-3

*Figure 2.1* The Continuous Circle

next game. New investors who have just acquired a football club often want to please the fans or make a statement to gain media attention and be loved. It is a form of ostentatious display of their wealth and power. An example is the -€543,66m net transfer balance of Chelsea FC in the season of 2022–2023 after the acquisition was led by Todd Boehly (Transfermarkt, 2023).

Is there a different way for a new investor to impact the football club while controlling the risks better? Starting within the Continuous Circle at the step, 'increase brand awareness' is a much smarter strategy. The club's reach will increase with limited financial investments and more fans will be recruited. It is a more sustainable way to build a football club step by step through brand management. Ultimately, if we follow the Continuous Circle, the result will be the same: sporting success. It might take a longer time, but it will be less artificial, more sustainable in the long term, and with fewer risks from a financial point of view.

Another question we must ask ourselves is: if the football industry is as big as the media suggests. The media often says it's a multibillion-dollar business, with too much money involved in football. They love publishing transfer fees and wages of players as clickbait to sell more copies or get more viewers. Therefore, is the football industry that big? No, it's not. If you compare the numbers hereunder, you'll understand why (Table 2.1).

Table 2.1 Economic Importance

| Combined professional clubs | Royal Dutch Shell |
|---|---|
| • England 1st & 2nd division<br>• France 1st & 2nd division<br>• Italy 1st & 2nd division<br>• Spain 1st division<br>• Netherlands 1st division<br>• Belgium 1st division | |
| Total companies: 180 | 1 |
| Total revenues: ± €14,5 Billion | €305 Billion |
| Difference: ±21 times less than Royal Dutch Shell | |

Source: Courtesy of Peeters (2018).

If we calculate all revenues from every football club in nine leagues, the total revenues of those 180 football clubs are still 21 times smaller than Royal Dutch Shell: a company in the energy and petrochemical industry. It brings a different perspective to media articles saying how big the football industry is. Nevertheless, football's impact on many people's daily lives cannot be underestimated.

Suppose football clubs want to grow their revenues or brand value to a similar level as Royal Dutch Shell, we recommend approaching the Continuous Circle from a different angle, similar to what other businesses do: brand positioning.

The greater the level of sporting competitiveness within a league, the more effort the club must exert to excel. To do that, they must invest wisely and start building a sustainable and broader business model. Thinking outside the box and doing things differently than all other football clubs will be vital in building a sustainable environment that does not always come down to the game's sporting aspect.

## Key takeaways

- The football industry is not as big as the media often implies.
- Creating a sustainable business model for the football club is key.
- Sporting results are important, but on-pitch success usually comes with a clear off-pitch strategy.

- If football clubs have the objective to become similar in size to non-football companies, such as Royal Dutch Shell, non-sporting growth strategies will have to be implemented.

# References

Peeters, T. (2018). Erasmus University.
Transfermarkt. (2023). Retrieved from: Transfermarkt: Transfermarkt.be

# 3 | Business models

A business model defines the operations of a football club. This has mainly to do with the ambitions and vision of the owner. Which goals or targets have been set for the short and the long term on the football side and – as important to strategy – on the investors' side?

There may be diverging views on whether profit-making should be the aim of a football club, as many believe that the club should serve the community. Nevertheless, the community plays a crucial role in the success of a football club. In order to not only fulfil sporting goals but also to survive, profit-making and revenue maximisation should be high on the to-do list. The higher the revenues, the higher the increase in quality of players will be, and the faster sporting success will come. Sporting success will be a factor in the increase of ticket sales, sponsorship, media, and merchandising. However, it will also develop the geographical area from which you attract fans, eventually increasing your fan base and market potential.

Important note: sustainability and the independence from the owner are crucial in the long term. Often clubs only – or to a very large extent – focus on sporting results to grow and, as a result, overspend to win more matches and gain sporting success. Add this up with a situation where an owner who year-in-year-out spends a fortune filling up the depths and then suddenly quits investing. As you can imagine, this is not so sustainable, right? What would happen if football clubs focussed more on generating commercial revenues while staying loyal to their identity? Instead of depending only on sporting results, football clubs should focus on the business elements within their control and mitigate against those not directly impressionable. Therefore, my advice is 'Yes, football should be at the centre of the club's

DOI: 10.4324/9781003312680-4

operations. However, do not only rely on it. Use it as your main product and activate the multiple products via a long-term business strategy'.

Various 'products or assets' can be commercialised in and around a football club. Currently, the men's first team and the stadium are the biggest sources of revenue. However, all other products are also important within the entire ecosystem that drives the football business. Often combinations of these products generate the highest revenues. For example, an academy player performs well in the U21 team, is promoted to the first team, and is later sold as a 'home-grown player' to a bigger team. Alternatively, look at how a community trust can create a deep connection among fans, increasing multiple revenue streams such as ticketing and merchandise.

Different 'products/assets' a football club has to offer:

- First team
- U21 team
- Women's team
- Academy
- Community trust
- eSports
- Stadium and other infrastructure
- Web3 (Club tokens or NFTs [Non-Fungible Tokens])
- Social media channels
- Retail channels such as merchandise

## The five business models in football

There are five different business models that football club owners try to follow. It does not matter at which level your club is playing; you will be able to see similarities within your club's strategy with one of the business models explained hereunder. Each business model has a different approach and a different end goal. Therefore, the football club's impact on the community and its fans is also very different.

### 1. Profit-maximising owner
*Arsenal FC*
Focus on generating as much revenue as possible and limit investments to ensure the net result stays positive over a long period. One of

the best examples representing this model is Arsenal FC in 2015–2020. Although Arsenal FC booked a loss of 30.6 million EURO in the season 2018/2019, the club's financial result over the previous five years was positive (Arsenal Football Club, 2019). The loss in the 18/19 season could be explained by the following:

- Overall operating profits were impacted by continued investment in player wages, which meant that total staff costs, excluding exceptional costs, grew by £8.4 million to £231.7 million in the financial year 2019 (2018 – £223.3 million).
- During the 2018–2019 season, exceptional costs incurred of £3.9 million compared to £17.2 million in the previous season, which was attributable to several changes in the first-team coaching and support personnel and transaction advisory costs incurred by the company in relation to KSE (Kroenke Sports & Entertainment) UK Inc becoming the group's sole shareholder.
- Profits were adversely impacted by participation in the UEFA Europa League as opposed to the more lucrative UEFA Champions League.
- Net interest costs were impacted by a negative movement of £0.7 million (£3.3 million positive in 2018) in the market value of the Group's Stadium Finance interest rate swap.

The Arsenal Group's profit for:

- The 2015/2016 year after taxation was 3.3 million EURO
- The 2016/2017 year after taxation was 50.4 million EURO
- The 2017/2018 year after taxation was 63.9 million EURO

(Arsenal FC, 2016; 2017; 2018)

For 2019/2020, Arsenal FC saw increased commercial revenues from adidas and the renewed deal with Emirates. However, another season outside the Champions League will continue to apply pressure on their financial results.

The result of this strategy is that the club mainly invests in younger players to not overspend on transfer fees but also to keep the wages at a lower rate. Young players take time to rise to the same competitive level as their main rival teams, and therefore, Arsenal has been missing out on playing European football in the past few years. From a business perspective, we can only support this model as it creates sustainability and a healthy situation for the club. From a sporting point of view, not playing European football regularly nor competing for the trophies at the end of the season impacts the club's overall growth and popularity. We recently noticed a change in strategy at the club with big investments in buying players. This might be why Arsenal FC had a net transfer balance of −£97.4M in the summer transfer window of 2022.

Another good example of this business model is Tottenham Hotspur. Their operational profits before player trading in the period before COVID-19 was £147.8M in 2019, £151.9M in 2018, £81.4M in 2017, £47.3M in 2016, and £34M in 2015. Even after player trading and taxation, they made a cumulative profit of £260M between 2015 and 2019. The opening of their new stadium will only increase their operational profit further (Tottenham Hotspur, 2019).

## 2. Win-maximising owner

*Paris Saint-Germain*

Winning at all costs with a focus on the men's first team is the strategy of club owners focussed on win-maximising. These clubs are characterised by their performance-based structure. Everyone within the organisation is focused on winning the domestic league title, the cup, and the European club competitions. The best example is Paris Saint-Germain. Founded in 1970, PSG is a very young club that has undergone several ownership changes. The last one is the most important; in 2012, the State of Qatar, through its shareholding organisation Qatar Sports Investments (QSI), became the club's sole owner. Upon their arrival, QSI pledged to form a team capable of winning the UEFA Champions League and making the club France's biggest asset. Consequently, since the summer of 2011, Paris Saint-Germain has spent over €1billion on player transfers such as Thiago Silva, Zlatan Ibrahimović, Edinson Cavani, David Luiz, Neymar, and Kylian Mbappé (Transfermarkt, 2022). These massive expenditures have translated into PSG's domination of French football, winning 20 national titles in the process. However, they have not yet brought home the coveted Champions League trophy, and this proud club has experienced problems with UEFA and its Financial Fair Play regulations (FFP). As of the 2018–2019 season, Paris Saint-Germain had the fifth-highest revenue in the footballing world with an annual turnover of €542M according to Deloitte, and is the world's eleventh most valuable football club, worth €825M according to Forbes. PSG's strong financial position has been sustained by the club's lucrative sponsorship deals with several commercial partners, including top sponsors Nike and ALL. Throughout its history, though, PSG has rarely been profitable. Before the Qatar buyout, the club's cumulative losses between 1998 and 2010 amounted to €300M (Paris Saint-Germain, 1998; 2010).

It is only logical that in a sport such as football, where money plays such an important role, sporting success follows when you spend more money. The more money invested, the better the players you can attract to your football club. The better players you have, the greater the likelihood of winning games. However, money is not everything in football; we have seen that before. There are several examples, such as Leicester City FC winning the Premier League. Buying the best players in the world still does not guarantee to win the biggest competitions, as has been proved by Paris Saint-Germain. Thankfully, the sport is still unpredictable, and football miracles still happen.

### 3. Benefactor owner
*Brighton & Hove Albion FC*

The benefactor owner can be seen as a very affluent person who has made a lot of money, enjoys being in the spotlight, and wants to give something back to the (local) community. The 'one who does good' and also invests in a football club. In the modern game, many of the more traditional kinds of benefactors still exist (but often in the smaller leagues), providing funds for what, in effect, is their 'trophy club'. Although it is easy to see how this can benefit the football club, it can also carry implicit dangers in the long term. What happens if the benefactor leaves? (Chadwick & Hamil, 2010)

Each of you can probably think of at least one unfortunate situation like this one, no matter where you come from. There are numerous cases of football investments gone wrong because the benefactor had no idea what they were doing but had a heart for the club. Eventually, in most cases, this led to the sale of the club, most likely after relegation.

Can a benefactor have a positive impact on the club? Absolutely, YES! We take Brighton & Hove Albion FC as an example, in which Tony Bloom acquired the club in 2009. Born and raised in Brighton, he saw an opportunity to invest in his childhood favourite football club, where his grandfather was vice-chairman during the 1970s. He secured a 75% shareholding in the club and invested over £93 million in the development of the new Falmer Stadium (Hayward, 2009). He led the team from Football League

One (third division) back to the Premier League in 2017 and turned it into a sustainable mid-table club in the Premier League. The club has increased its revenues significantly and is on its way to becoming a more financial sustainable club. Even though this has been a wonderful success story so far, it started from a benefactor perspective. Let us hope that Mr. Bloom does not turn his back on the club any time soon as the club still lists in 2022 in the top 20 European clubs with the biggest net debt.

## 4. Socially responsible owner

*Forest Green Rovers*

In this model, the main motivation to run a football club is not based on on-field performances. These football clubs will not be lifting trophies one year after the other but are conscious of their social role in society. A positive impact on the community and their focus on the overall strategy is key. One of the best examples is Forest Green Rovers, currently playing in the English League Two. FIFA recently described this club as the greenest football club in the world. It is the world's first vegan club. The stadium is powered with 100% renewable energy; they play on a pitch free from pesticides and irrigated with rainwater, and the team jerseys are made 50% out of bamboo to replace plastic. Furthermore, in 2018, it became the world's first United Nations-certified carbon-neutral football club. Forest Green Rovers plans to build the world's greenest stadium, the so-called 'Eco Park', fully surrounded by 500 trees and 1.8 km of hedgerows to promote biodiversity.

This is their statement on their website:

> We focus on the three biggest contributing sectors; Energy, Transport, and Food – which account for most of everybody's personal carbon footprint. These are the focus of our business activities in terms of providing solutions and alternatives – they are also the focus of our communications, which is a key way we seek to bring change. This is also our focus when looking at the environmental impact of our activities.
>
> (Forest Green Rovers, 2022)

The result of this business model is that the fans should not get their hopes up for being promoted to the Premier League any time soon or winning trophies such as the cup or league title. The main priority is sustainable financial management focusing on society and the community.

## 5. Marketing owner

*FC Red Bull Salzburg, New York Red Bulls*

This is one of the best-known business models in the football industry. A marketing owner buys a football club to generate visibility for his main brand and turn the spotlights towards the mother company. Whether the true purpose of these investments is a new product launch, making powerful connections with politicians, or integrating your brand in new target markets, the football club generates the necessary media attention to complete the main objectives. The best and most well-known example is Red Bull.

The Red Bull brand is everywhere, and Red Bull's brand is what drives the company. Red Bull is headquartered in Austria, so it would not be a surprise if they sponsored a local football club. However, they have taken it way beyond that with the acquisition of New York Red Bull, FC Red Bull Salzburg, RB Leipzig, and Red Bull Bragantino. Their football franchises, owned and sponsored football clubs, brand's profile. Over time, Red Bull have diversified beyond being a drink manufacturer and retailer by investing in other industries such as sport, entertainment, music, and events. One of these developments led to the creation of the Red Bull Media House.

# Closing

There is no right or wrong ownership strategy, but fans must understand that the club's objectives will differ for each different owner type. Whenever an investor wants to acquire a football club, it is important to know if fans would accept the investor's objectives. It can lead to fan protest and frustration if there is a mismatch. Before acquiring a football club, decent research is important to minimise investment risks and avoid implementing a business model that does not fit the local community. Aside from the different business models in football, there are four reasons why investors acquire football clubs. They invest either out of love for the club or the game itself, for a return on investment, out of vanity or insanity.

Recently, we have seen the development of multi-club ownership structures. This means that a football club or holding company owns multiple football clubs. The leading examples within such a structure are City Football Group and Red Bull, both organisations owning multiple football clubs worldwide. As discussed earlier, Red Bull's strategy is based on marketing, while City Football Group has a special combination of strategies. Conversely, they have a win-maximising strategy with their flagship football clubs like Manchester City FC, New York City FC, Melbourne City FC, and Mumbai City FC. Their strategy at smaller football clubs such as Lommel SK or Montevideo City FC is completely different. They focus on talent development to find the next special talent for one of their clubs. Of course, player trading at that level can be very profitable and help support the group's finances. Nevertheless, another key strategy of the holding company is profit-maximising based on a very long-term plan. Capturing data from fans in key markets such as the USA, India, Australia, China, and Europe plays a major role in the strategy to increase the enterprise valuation and attract new investors, as we have seen with Silver Lake Partners.

## Key takeaways

- The ownership type has a strong impact on the club's vision and operations.
- There is no right or wrong, but not every ownership type fits every football club.
- Focus on creating revenue streams from assets you can control the best.
- Stay loyal to your objectives as an investor and do not start to mix your models.

## References

Arsenal FC. (2016; 2017; 2018). *Financial Statement*. Arsenal.

Arsenal Football Club. (2019). *Financial Statement*. Arsenal.

Chadwick, S., & Hamil, S. (2010). *In Managing Football*. Routledge.

Forest Green Rovers. (2022). *Another-Way*. Retrieved from Forest Green Rovers: https://www.fgr.co.uk/another-way

Hayward, P. (2009, May 19). Boom's Cash Injection Can Make Brighton Blossom Again. *The Guardian*.

Paris Saint-Germain. (1998; 2010). *Financial Statements*.

Tottenham Hotspur. (2019). *Retrieved from Tottenham Hotspur Annual Accounts*. Retrieved from: https://www.tottenhamhotspur.com/media/28139/tottenham-hotspur-limited-signed-accounts-30-6-19.pdf

Transfermarkt. (2022). https://www.transfermarkt.be/fc-paris-saint-germain/alletransfers/verein/583

# 4    Revenue generation
## Simon Van Kerckhoven and Martijn Ernest

As this book focuses on bringing a football club towards commercial success, we will not discuss youth and talent development or selling players as a revenue generation model for a football club. Income from transfers is not recurrent and not a stable revenue channel, nor is it qualifying for European club competitions. Will transfers and European club competitions benefit a football club's income statement? Absolutely! Are there many clubs that currently use this as their main source of income? Absolutely! Are there clubs that faced financial problems due to this strategy? Absolutely! Make sure that, as a club, you treat this revenue stream as an add-on. As an extra which is not included in your annual budget.

We can categorise football club recurrent revenues into three main categories:

1. **Venue:** Ticketing, Hospitality, food, beverages, and rent.
2. **Commercial:** Sponsorship, merchandise, licensing, social media, Web3
3. **Broadcast:** National and international broadcasting rights, club TV, documentary

Ideally, there is a balance between these three revenue streams. That way, when an unforeseen event hits one revenue stream, the impact will be less. An example of where this went wrong is the change in the TV contract in Ligue 1 in the summer of 2020 owing to the COVID-19 pandemic. Many French clubs faced huge losses as they were dependent on the financial income from broadcasting.

DOI: 10.4324/9781003312680-5

**Club revenue perfection**

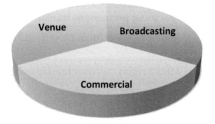

■ Broadcasting   ■ Commercial   ■ Venue

*Figure 4.1* Club revenue perfection

**Club revenue imperfection**

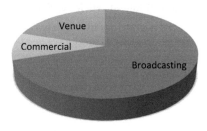

■ Broadcasting   ■ Commercial   ■ Venue

*Figure 4.2* Club revenue imperfection

Most clubs work towards a perfect income balance but struggle to achieve the perfect mix. A reliance on broadcast revenues is the most common struggle, and some clubs even completely rely on broadcasting revenues (Figures 4.1 and 4.2).

The European Club Association's revenue model, explained in their ECA (European Club Association) Football Management Guide, describes the differences between short-term, medium-term, and long-term revenue streams (European Club Association, 2018). This gives a good overview but it is not the only way a revenue model must be built up. It is up to the club to find strategic applications within its identified market, geographic location, and asset range. Hereunder, you can find a list of different revenue streams, sorted from short-term to long-term sustainability (Tables 4.1–4.3).

Table 4.1 Short-Term Revenue Streams

| Transfers of players | Outgoing permanent transfers and loans |
|---|---|
| European competition revenues | Media rights & prize money UEFA Club competitions |
| Domestic club competition revenues | Media rights national league and domestic cup |
| Matchday revenues | Ticketing, stadium retail catering, hospitality, and others |
| Non-matchday revenues | Conferences, events, commercial floor space, concerts, museums, and others |

Table 4.2 Medium-Term Revenue Streams

| Merchandising | Commercial sale of articles with club-identifying features |
|---|---|
| Co-branding | Marketing campaigns in which two or more brands are combined in order to produce a positive commercial return |
| Sponsorship | Technical, institutional, commercial, and ownership-linked endorsements |

Table 4.3 Long-Term Revenue Streams

| Membership fees | Customer/fan retention |
|---|---|
| Business clubs | Initiatives that run in tandem with the club's matchday hospitality and sponsorship operations |
| Institutional contributions | The financial relationship between the club, the state, and local authorities |
| Naming rights | Commercialisation of the club's infrastructure (stadium, training centre, and youth academy) |

# Revenue optimisation vs. revenue utilisation

You will have noticed that my approach is based on long-term and sustainable management strategies aimed at slowly but steadily professionalising the football club in each department with a clear growth plan and clear objectives in place. In many football clubs, management teams tend to gamble on sporting success as they would like to prove themselves to the owner. Sporting Directors and Chief Executive Officers decide to invest most of the budget in buying new players in the hope of sporting success in the fastest way possible. Furthermore, they blame the coach for saving themselves if it goes wrong.

These football clubs often rely on transfer fees, prize money from UEFA club competitions, and subsidies. However, these revenue streams are non-controllable, non-recurrent, and therefore non-sustainable pillars to make up a pre-season budget estimation. That is exactly why I do not include these revenue streams in the operational budget of a football club. These incomes can be used for good effects, like investments in the academy, infrastructure, community, or fan activations. It is also why I do not include outgoing transfer fees, loans, and sell-on options as an expense. These expenses should be monitored, controlled, and managed, but it is not recurrent operational cost.

The transfer revenues from selling players should only be partially reinvested in new players. Many incoming transfer fees should be invested in sustainable growth strategies such as developing the commercial team, marketing and communication departments, infrastructure, and the youth academy. Success in football club management is not always determined by having the highest revenues, as real success depends on how you use those revenues for growth purposes.

Therefore, I strongly advise football clubs that do not have a win-maximising business model – like Paris Saint-Germain – to invest, grow, and optimise controllable, sustainable, and recurrent revenue streams. Furthermore, even at PSG, there was the development of the commercial team to optimise the commercial revenues of the club.

Revenue optimisation means optimising all the revenue streams for the football club. Revenue utilisation means all the costs it has or how a football club uses its financial resources. We will discuss this further in this chapter regarding financial management, but hereunder, you can already find an overview.

## Revenue Optimisation

One of the revenue streams that are not often discussed in the media is competition revenues. This revenue is guaranteed as it relates to the league's domestic broadcasting income.

Other revenues on matchday are ticketing, food and beverage, B2C (single tickets and season tickets), ticketing B2B, hospitality B2B, merchandising, matchday activations such as photo booths or the lottery, and advertisements like one such as ball sponsors or giveaways.

On non-matchdays, the different revenue streams are endless. However, we will list a few such as events (conferences, concerts), commercial floor space renting (office space, retail stores), museums, partnerships, licensing (other brands may use the club logo), membership fees, business clubs, institutional contributions (government), new business development (non-football-related investments such as real estate and marketing agencies), eSports, financial income and media (online, offline, and social media), and digital such as NFT's (Non-Fungible Tokens) and fan tokens.

Some potential extra revenue streams are not recurrent but depend on the sporting performances of the club. These revenues would be a bonus. For example, the annual budget of the football club Bate Borisov is 7 million euros, and the club from Belarus plays in a country with limited influence in Europe. The broadcasting funds are very low, as is the income from sponsorship compared to bigger leagues in Spain, England, or France. But the champion of Belarus also has a chance at UEFA Champions League football. Owing to the qualifications they need to play, such revenues cannot be budgeted for due to uncertainty. Moreover, given the historical data, it is even more unlikely that the club would go beyond the group stage in the Champions League upon qualification. So, you should never include such revenues in your budget predictions if there is a big uncertainty in receiving the income. However, that does not mean that you cannot use the income for various projects, in case of success. Examples of potential extra revenues are:

- UEFA competitions revenues (prize money and broadcasting revenue through the Champions League, European League, or Conference League)
- Domestic competitions revenues (prize money from national competition or the national cup)

## Revenue Utilisation

Revenue Utilisation means how a football club's budget is spent. The highest cost is the remuneration for players and staff, which includes salary and employee benefit expenses such as accommodation, transport, and meal vouchers.

From a logistic point of view, the club has travel costs, catering, kit, or clothing, medical costs, administration, and IT. Consider costs like catering, security, and attributes on matchdays and events. Infrastructure and maintenance are often also a high cost owing to the constant need for improvements. Furthermore, you have taxes, marketing, communication, human resources, the youth academy, and corporate social responsibility.

In chapter 11, "Financial management," I have explained the various costs of managing a football club in a more detailed way.

# Changing environment

When you make a strategic plan, consider the brand, the financial income, and the associated costs. Where do we want to go, and when do we succeed? However, keep in mind that the world is not standing still and the sporting environment may change for your club season after season.

When an investor arrives at a football club, they often want to impress the fans with some big-name transfers and spend a lot of money. We understand that sporting investments sometimes must be made to accelerate sporting ambitions. Nevertheless, as maybe the most important saying in finances indicates: 'Never spend money you do not have'. This might not be the best long-term strategy. It is important that management teams stick to the original strategy and do not panic when sporting results are worse than expected.

Having a plan for relegation or promotion could offer some calmness in the organisation so that, in case this happens, you do not make any irrational decisions because of time pressure. The Royal Dutch Football Association – KNVB's knowledge centre has developed a guide for management teams of those clubs facing a potential relegation or promotion. The KNVB has created three different levels a football club can be involved with around promotion or relegation, which are explained hereunder (KNVB Expertise, 2019a).

- **Structural:** continuously considering promotion or relegation.
  - How will we make use of means and people?
  - **Period:** 1–3 years
- **Strategic:** Broadly considering promotion or relegation when it becomes a realistic possibility.
  - What do we do internally to create a new external direction?
  - **Period:** 3–5 years

- **Operational:** Implementing necessary changes after actual promotion or relegation.
  - Making use of building blocks (ticketing, sponsoring, merchandising)
  - **Period:** Less than one year

It is generally advised to take a structural promotion or relegation into account. Not in day-to-day operations, but for example, when concluding contracts. Examples are clauses in employment contracts, sponsorship contracts, and leasing of exploitation rights. Annoying situations can be prevented by including protected clauses.

Several clubs face a possible promotion or relegation during the season, with the risk becoming more concrete during the season. When a potential promotion or relegation becomes a serious option, the consequences will have to be considered strategically and operationally.

Clubs that are promoted or relegated go through a process that can be divided into four stages (Table 4.4).

Working with a shadow budget is recommended structurally to respond to any promotion or relegation. The possible promotion or relegation scenarios must be included in this shadow budget. Suppose a professional football club must submit a budget, it must be submitted to the licensing committee of the football league. In the Netherlands, this is no later than April 8 (a similar date as the budget submission to UEFA), before the new season starts. However, as football competitions only end around the end of May, a club normally will not know whether promotion/relegation is a fact until then. A shadow budget prevents being surprised by sporting results. The valuable time gained with this can then be immediately used with other matters related to promotion or relegation (KNVB Expertise, 2019b).

*Table 4.4* **Phases of Promotion and Relegation Management**
(Courtesy of KNVB Expertise, 2019a)

| 1. Expectation | 2. Processing | 3. Preparation | 4. Translation |
|---|---|---|---|
| Period: Winter break – end of the competition | Period: First weeks after promotion/relegation | Period: End of the season until the start of the new season | Period: Start new season |
| Elaborate scenarios and action plan | Working out an action plan and determining deadlines | Implementing the action plan and preparing for the start of the competition | Implement operational adjustments |

# The ultimate goal

The entire sports environment, emotions, and passions come forth from striving for success. In this book, 'Leadership for commercial success', we explain how football clubs can increase revenue streams and become part of the continuous circle towards sporting success and brand awareness. Nevertheless, club owners have an underlying objective to increase their brand awareness: enterprise value.

The enterprise value measures the total worth of a company's core business, regardless of how that company is financed. This is particularly relevant in football, where clubs are financed differently. Brand Finance, the brand valuation consultancy firm, created a league-specific revenue multiple based on various data. The league revenue multiple is adjusted based on seven relevant factors that influence a club's enterprise value: league perceptions, stadium ownership, squad value, brand strength, global reach of the fanbase, club heritage, and operating margin (Brand Finance, 2022a; Table 4.5).

Brand strength is most directly and easily impacted by on-pitch performance, advertising, and brand management. Three key areas are analysed to determine the strength of a brand: investment, brand equity, and their impact on business performance. It is the impact of a brand on its stakeholders (Brand Finance, 2022b; Table 4.6).

*Table 4.5* Brand Finance, Football 50 Ranking, Enterprise Value

| 2022 Rank | Brand | 2022 Brand enterprise value (M) | Enterprise value change (%) |
|---|---|---|---|
| 1 | FC Bayern Munich | €4,736 | +32.3 |
| 2 | Real Madrid CF | €3,593 | +0.6 |
| 3 | Liverpool FC | €3,592 | +8.5 |
| 4 | Manchester City FC | €3,442 | +19.7 |
| 5 | Manchester United FC | €3,428 | +12.1 |
| 6 | Paris Saint-Germain | €3,365 | +14.6 |
| 7 | FC Barcelona | €3,032 | +7.2 |
| 8 | Chelsea FC | €2,660 | +10.1 |
| 9 | Juventus FC | €2,294 | +33.3 |
| 10 | Arsenal FC | €1,746 | −2.4 |

Brand valuation is a calculation that understands 'brand value' as the net economic benefit a licensor would derive from licensing the brand in the open market. The value of a brand includes intangible assets such as names, logos, terms, signs, designs, and the associated marketing within the brand's business (Table 4.7).

In 2022, we witnessed the rebirth of AC Milan as the fastest-growing football brand in the world. AC Milan has a rich history but has not been performing in the past decade. Elliott Investment Management brought the

*Table 4.6* Brand Finance, Football 50 Ranking, Brand Strength Index Score

| 2022 Rank | Brand | 2022 Brand strength index score | Brand strength change (%) |
|---|---|---|---|
| 1 | Real Madrid CF | 94.0 | +2.7 |
| 2 | Liverpool FC | 92.9 | +3.9 |
| 3 | FC Barcelona | 92.1 | +1.0 |
| 4 | Manchester United FC | 92.0 | +3.3 |
| 5 | FC Bayern Munich | 88.6 | −3.3 |
| 6 | Manchester City FC | 87.7 | +1.6 |
| 7 | Juventus FC | 86.1 | +2.4 |
| 8 | Arsenal FC | 85.9 | +2.8 |
| 9 | Chelsea FC | 84.7 | −1.6 |
| 10 | Tottenham Hotspur FC | 83.1 | −1.7 |

*Table 4.7* Brand Finance, Football 50 Ranking, Brand Value

| 2022 Rank | Brand | 2022 Brand value (m) | Brand value change (%) |
|---|---|---|---|
| 1 | Real Madrid CF | €1,525 | +19.5 |
| 2 | Manchester City FC | €1,327 | +18.7 |
| 3 | FC Barcelona | €1,325 | +4.6 |
| 4 | Liverpool FC | €1,272 | +30.7 |
| 5 | Manchester United FC | €1,250 | +10.6 |
| 6 | FC Bayern Munich | €1,109 | +3.8 |
| 7 | Paris Saint-Germain | €1,027 | +15.7 |
| 8 | Tottenham Hotspur FC | €873 | +20.7 |
| 9 | Chelsea FC | €855 | +11.1 |
| 10 | Arsenal FC | €793 | +17.5 |

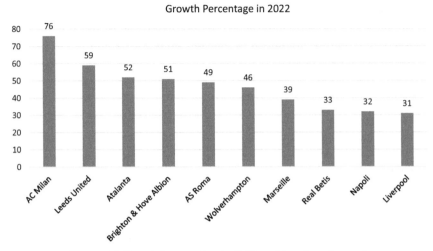

Figure 4.3 Brand finance, football 50 ranking, brand growth

club back to its first Serie A title in 2022 since 2011 and later sold it to Red-Bird Capital Partners with a club valuation of €1.2 billion (AC Milan, 2022; Figure 4.3).

In 49th place, we find Flamengo, the first and only non-European team in the top 50, with a brand value of €96 million. They are alongside Celtic FC (brand value of €113 million), AFC Ajax (brand value of €182 million), and SL Benfica (brand value of €101 million), the only four clubs from outside the 'Big Five' leagues.

The enterprise valuation is considered when a football club is sold or acquired. According to Forbes Roman, Abramovich was asking £3 billion for the shares of Chelsea FC, while the club had an enterprise value of £2.31 billion in 2021. Eventually, the club was sold for £2.5 billion with an additional obliged investment of £1.75 billion over the next ten years. The fact that such a big football club rarely becomes available on the market increased the price even more (Forbes, 2022).

## Key takeaways

- Build sustainable and balanced commercial revenue streams.
- Control your costs.
- Create a strategic plan and do not panic after less fortunate sporting results.

- Most investors seek sporting success to drive revenue growth, while they should focus more on improving the brand and enterprise value.
- Seven factors that influence brand and enterprise value. Only two of them are sport-related.

# References

AC Milan. (2022, June 1). *News*. Retrieved from AC Milan: https://www.acmilan.com/en/news/articles/club/2022-06-01/redbird-capital-partners-enters-into-agreement-with-elliott-advisors-to-acquire-ac-milan

Brand Finance. (2022a). *Football 50 Ranking*. Brand Finance.

Brand Finance. (2022b). *Football 50 Ranking Brand Value*. Brand Finance.

European Club Association. (2018). ECA Club Management Guide. In O. Jarosz, *ECA Club Management Guide*. European Club Association.

Forbes. (2022, May 9). Retrieved from: Forbes https://www.forbes.com/sites/mike-ozanian/2022/05/09/chelsea-fc-valued-at-309-billion-in-sale-to-group-led-by-todd-boehly/

KNVB Expertise. (2019a). *Handboek Promotie & Degradatie Betaald Voetbal*. KNVB. https://fbo.nl/wp-content/uploads/2019/02/2018-Handboek-promotie-degradatie-definitief.pdf

KNVB Expertise. (2019b). *Handboek Promotie & Degradatie Management Betaald Voetbal*. KNVB.

PART

# Organisational structure of a football club

# 5

# Introduction human resources in football business

The COVID pandemic had a huge impact on the world in general. The geopolitical, supply chain, and energy crisis that followed in 2022 created a terrible situation for many people and organisations. Often, people forget that football clubs also face these challenges despite of their big investments and activities in the transfer market. The reason for this is not difficult to determine. In the summer of 2022, during the energy crisis and the war in Ukraine, many football fans struggled to pay their bills as life got expensive. Nevertheless, the net transfer spending by football clubs in the Premier League exceeded £1 billion for the first time in a transfer window.

Even though the global energy crisis has not seemed to affect the football industry at the time of writing (apart from higher energy bill for operating the stadium and training centre), when it comes to welfare, human resource management, and a positive instructive environment, sporting organisations still have much to learn. Over the past few years, I have often spoken to those in my network working at football clubs and concluded that there still is a top-down culture in most football clubs, meaning that the executive management does not listen to their employees. We call this an authoritarian management style, often implemented by the owner or CEO and creating a disrupted organisational culture. Furthermore, there are other issues that we see in sporting organisations. There is a sincere lack of long-term recruitment strategy for non-sporting staff.

The labour force is changing in an ever more complex job market, but the human resource management methods stuck in our management systems are not undergoing the same evolution. This creates many challenges and opportunities to take the lead on competitors or catch up. One of the questions football clubs need to ask themselves is whether they are missing the

DOI: 10.4324/9781003312680-7

opportunities and possibilities to hire the best talent. Because the world is getting more dynamic, international, and unpredictable, there is a need to think further outside the box regarding the quest for talent.

Research shows us that the biggest concern of CEOs is the availability of the right talent in time (The Conference Board, 2019). Brands are entering sports sponsorship to become more likeable and attractive for talent recruitment. However, what or who is a 'talent'? Having the right competencies for doing the job is one criterion. However, other necessary characteristics are maybe even more crucial. Those characteristics are having a cultural fit with the organisation, feeling connected to the mission and vision of an organisation, being available, and having the ability to embed quickly in the company. The mindset of an employee is much more important than their skills, as skills can be taught but a mindset is difficult to change.

As Steven Bartlett, host of the Podcast 'The Diary of a CEO', explained so well in an interview, 'The quality of your talent will be the single biggest prediction for your outcome. You are a recruitment company, and this is a talent war' (Steven Bartlett, 2021). There has been a big shift in the recruitment world when moving to a candidate-driven market. There are simply more jobs available than candidates, giving job seekers a higher level of power and flexibility. However, it is not just a case of filling open positions; it is a case of having those roles filled with talent. To attract talent is to create an environment where they can be themselves and flourish. Employees should not feel constantly watched or controlled to be caught when they make a mistake; they should feel empowered and served by the senior management team. Great leaders are responsible for the people responsible for the jobs within an organisation, not the job itself (Simon Sinek, 2016). Companies focussed in the past years on filling the fridge with lemonade to create a better working environment. These small, odd perks are a simple gift to improve employees' morale. Companies have spent a lot of money in the past decade on workplace improvements to attract young talent. Think about ping-pong tables, nearly free lunches, or even massages and yoga classes. However, research shows that companies should invest more in training management teams to communicate better and respectfully and nurture employee well-being. Employees do not want to contribute just to the bottom of the organisation but also to its purpose.

So, what is the solution? Most of the problems arise from the fact that there is a skills gap in the team or in an organisation. Because the world is never standing still and always evolving, investing in the training and development of employees and management needs to be addressed.

## Key takeaways

- The war on talent in football happens in player recruitment and in a football club's operational and commercial department.
- Clubs should invest more in training the management executives to communicate better and more respectfully with their staff.
- When football clubs have a staff turnover issue, it is because employees do not feel validated and respected enough for the work they do.

## References

Bartlett, S. (2021, December 3). *War on Talent*. Retrieved from lxahub: https://www.lxahub.com/stories/steven-bartlett-on-the-talent-war

The Conference Board. (2019). *C-Suite-Outlook*. Retrieved from Conference-board: https://www.conference-board.org/topics/c-suite-outlook

Sinek, S. (2016). Most Leaders Don't Even Know The Game They're In. *YouTube*.

# 6 | Human resource management

The human resource department is responsible for multiple things. However, the most important ones are maximising staff performance and supporting the management to create a thriving environment where everyone feels welcomed and respected. Other general HR (human resource) tasks, regarding compliance with legal obligations, employment, and labour laws, are essential. HR is also responsible for health and safety provisions within the organisation.

Additionally, appropriate staff recruitment and helping current employees and management grow through feedback and trainings are key. Many conflict issues among the staff can be resolved by listening to your current employees and the ones you are recruiting. Listen to their personal ambitions and where they see themselves within 10–15 years from now. Draft a career path with them with clear objectives, such as skills and knowledge that must be developed to grow to their dream position within the organisation.

An important part of maintaining continuity in an organisation is keeping your employees satisfied from a career perspective and an organisational culture point of view. Create a clear strategy for internal and external training programs such as courses, seminars, or workshops to challenge and improve the skills of your colleagues. An open and positive environment also helps for a positive feeling in the workplace. A work–life balance in a crazy entertainment industry such as football is necessary to prevent employees from getting a burn-out or even permanently leaving the organisation. In other industries, we have seen a new position within organisations – 'Chief Happiness Officer' – who looks at how they can reduce the absenteeism figures, for example, and act before problems arise. The aim is to put people in the right place and find a good match between their job

DOI: 10.4324/9781003312680-8

and what they like doing. That means that sometimes an employee must or can be reallocated to a new position within the company. Managers should be prepared to give or ask for feedback and not wait for a fixed evaluation moment. Communicating with each other daily significantly lowers the threshold for raising certain issues. Additionally, managers should regularly organise team events during working hours so employees can build and maintain a bond more easily with each other and the executive management team. Value little things as happiness is often found within obvious things. However, most importantly, employees should be appreciated for their work and commitment.

A company's culture is essential to its success. It shapes the way employees interact with each other, the way they approach work, and how they represent the organisation to the outside world. Unfortunately, certain behaviours can cause irreparable harm to a company's culture. These behaviours can be classified into five main categories.

1. The first category is a lack of trust. If employees do not trust the management team, or if the management team does not trust the employees, the company's culture can quickly deteriorate. Trust is essential for effective collaboration, and it allows employees to take risks and make mistakes without fear of retribution.
2. The second category is micromanagement. Micromanaging is a management style where managers closely oversee and control every aspect of their employees' work. This style of management can cause employees to feel undervalued as if their manager does not trust them to do their job effectively. This lack of trust can lead to demotivation and decreased productivity.
3. The third category is poor communication. When communication is lacking within an organisation, misunderstandings and frustrations can quickly arise. Employees may not know what is expected of them, leading to confusion and mistakes. Miscommunication can also lead to conflicts between co-workers, which can damage relationships and cause tension in the workplace.
4. The fourth category is a lack of transparency. Transparency is critical for building trust among employees. When employees are kept in the dark about important decisions or changes within the organisation, they may feel undervalued and unimportant. This can lead to a lack of motivation and decreased productivity.

37

5. Finally, negative behaviour should never be ignored. When negative behaviour is allowed to go unchecked, it can quickly spread throughout the organisation. This can lead to a toxic work environment, where employees do not feel safe or valued. Addressing negative behaviour promptly and effectively is essential for maintaining a healthy work culture.

In conclusion, understanding these five categories of behaviour that can harm a company's culture is essential for maintaining a positive work environment. By fostering trust, avoiding micromanagement, promoting clear communication, prioritising transparency, and addressing negative behaviour, companies can create a culture where employees feel valued, supported, and motivated to do their best work.

## Organisational structure fitting five business models

As each of the five business models we introduced has different objectives, the organisational structure will also be very different within other areas of the football club's business. Hereunder, we explain which departments' owners within each business model focus on the most and lay different accents. Note that there is no right or wrong and that every owner or director can implement their organisational structure. At the end of this chapter, you can find a visualised potential organisational structure for an average-sized club.

*Profit-maximising owner*

A profit-maximising owner is focussed on making as much profit as possible. Therefore, the organisation will be as lean as possible, with the absolute minimum number of employees necessary in each department to keep the costs low but with a high focus on the commercial and sporting departments to increase revenues. The different commercial departments, such as ticketing, events, merchandise, sponsorship, and hospitality, will have more sales managers than average. You will also see the importance of non-football data playing a big role in these football clubs as it will drive commercial revenue such as merchandise and sponsorship.

## Win-maximising owner

Win-maximising owners will focus more on the sporting side than the commercial departments. Some roles, such as data analysts, video analysts, and a wider medical and physical staff might not always be common in other football clubs. Mental coaches and nutritionists will also support the player squad and help them perform in the best circumstances. Of course, the absolute world's top football clubs, such as PSG and FC Barcelona, have excellent and very large commercial departments, as the more revenue they generate, the more they can invest in players. However, do not forget that also, in smaller leagues, there are clubs with a win-maximising owner and a less developed commercial department.

## Benefactor owner

Benefactor owners often invest little in human resources. They prefer a lean organisation that is easy to control and manage. They often work without a sporting director, so no one can interfere with player transfers and salary negotiations as they would like to do that themselves or at least be highly involved. Benefactors fear losing control of the organisation and want to be highly involved in each department. From case to case, they might also interfere with the coach, question his decisions, or even make kind suggestions on what the starting 11 should be. Additionally, you will only see the minimum of staff necessary in other departments. Benefactor owners are becoming very rare at the highest professional level in football. However, occasionally, they are very successful such as FC Sheriff from Transnistria, Moldavia, who qualified for the UEFA Champions League in 2021 and won their first two group matches.

## Socially responsible owner

Socially responsible owners care less about sporting performance than win-maximising owners. Therefore, they often need a sporting director, which may be the CEO and head coach making the sporting decisions. The commercial department needs to be strongly developed too. The focus is on the community and society, which will be strongly integrated into the club's organisational structure. Often, there will be a fan service or fan engagement manager to give extra attention and care to the well-being of their fans and community.

*Marketing owner*

Marketing owners care a lot about the brand and reputation of their football club, its reach, and media attention. Therefore, the marketing department will be fully developed with high investments in social media, content creation, and public relations. Equipped with the best brand directors, graphic designers, content creators, and communication specialists. As sporting performance often reflects a brand, the sporting department will also be well established but never the main or sole focus.

# Organisation chart of an average size football club

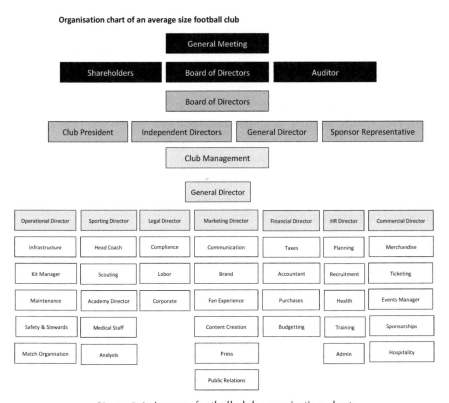

*Figure 6.1* Average football club organisation chart

# Key takeaways

- Implement a strong governance and recruitment strategy.
- Work with youngsters and provide them with a career plan and smart objectives for each possible promotion.
- Adjust your organisational chart to the business model and recruit first for the roles that impact that business model most.
- Do not be afraid to overpay slightly for quality and dare to invest in the education, training, and development of employees and the management team.
- Organisational culture has a big influence on staff turnover.

# PART

# III

# Strategic focus areas of football club management

Brand first! Whether you are new to the football club organisation or have worked there for many years, it does not matter. Defining the values and vision of a football club can only be done when you have thought about your football club's brand and the kind of brand you would like it to be.

This should be independent of the ownership model, the owner's ambitions, the board of directors, or investors. It is about balancing the important focus areas in football club management: sporting, commercial, and social. How can you make the most of the football club's brand story in your new position? And how can you take advantage of the football club's assets?

In this part of this book, we provide all the tools we consider important for each football club to follow the path to commercial success. We start this part with five strategic building blocks. Chapters 8–12 to ultimately determine a strategic plan which we will discuss in chapter 13 After the strategic plan has been drafted, we will discuss nine output functions in chapters 14–22 to activate the plan.

DOI: 10.4324/9781003312680-9

# 7 Brand identification

It does not matter whether you are already working at a football club or if you wish to develop your career towards a position in a football club, you want to be fully aware of everything that comes with the subject of brand identification, to know all the ins and outs about a football club's brand. Knowing all relevant information about the brand strategy of your employer will help you in any position you might have within the organisation. How can you use the football clubs in your new position optimally? From the fan DNA to the football philosophy, everything will be discussed. I will also show you an example of a strategic plan based on brand strategy. However, that will be for later; let us begin with the general brand identity of the sport football.

Football is intrinsically a love brand. A love brand, also known as a 'love mark', is an example of a brand that strongly appeals to consumers, making it preferable to other brands but 'loved'. Nutella and Coca-Cola are examples of typical worldwide famous love brands other than football.

In his book 'The Lovemarks Effect', Kevin Roberts explains the theory of three primary factors that make a brand a love brand: (Roberts, 2004)

1. **Mystery**
   Does the brand tell a story? Does the story inspire the consumers and even tempt them to dream?
2. **Sensuality**
   Can the brand be experienced with the senses? Does it have its own sound, a typical look, or a certain feeling?
3. **Intimacy**
   Can the customer build an emotional relationship with the brand through empathy, passion, and dedication?

DOI: 10.4324/9781003312680-10

How do these factors relate to football? The football career dreams we had when we were children, perhaps forming part of the 'mystery' factor of the brand story.

Every child dreamt of playing for his or her favourite football club. Playing in the shirt of your dream club, together with one of the idols who until then only hung as a poster on the bedroom door. The sensuality factor can be traced back to the experience of visiting the stadium on match day. The road to the stadium and the visit to the fan shop are all part of preparing for the match, seeing the players live, and hearing the fans sing the club chant in the stands. Sharing emotions in a win or a loss with thousands of other supporters are strongly related to the intimacy factor and being part of a club's supporters.

Before the commercialisation of professional football took off, clubs had already developed elements that confirmed their identity and made it unique compared to other football clubs. This started at every football club by using a unique name so that the teams could be separated on paper. On the field, the club colours ensured that both opponents did not look alike. Subsequently, club logos were designed and used to increase the recognisability further.

As football clubs evolved, they and their fans adopted songs to represent the club's values or to glorify on-field performances. Belgian football club KAA Gent, founded on 31 October 1900, is known as 'The Buffalo's'. The nickname originated from the American William Cody's, also known as Buffalo Bill, a circus where the audience was encouraged to scream 'Buffalo! Buffalo!'. Quickly, the hollo became popular among the students in Ghent. During the Olympic Games in Antwerp in 1920, KAA Gent athletics team member answered the American delegation's yelling with 'Buffalo! Buffalo!'. Together with that athlete, KAA Gent received the nickname, 'The Buffalo's' (KAA Gent, 2016). This shows that the identity of a football club can be formed in many ways and that its history plays a key role in its identification. It is not something you can integrate artificially.

It is clear that football brands have a strong historical value, but I believe this is not enough, and clubs should focus again on outing their unique identity in every possible way. For example, I use McDonald's, a globally known retail chain and brand offering more than just a meal. You can organise a birthday party for your child with all the trimmings. McDonald's does not only want to make the best food for you; this originally American company wants to make every customer in every store smile.

The Walt Disney Company is also an expert in offering experiences with the world-famous Disney theme parks. Workers are called actors, visitors are guests, and theme parks with multiple branches worldwide are the stage. However, Disney does not only want to offer the best entertainment in the world through its well-known theme parks, cruises, and more. Disney wants to give the customers memories forever. Memories of a period, however short, of pure happiness and joy (Roberts, 2004). The question I ask myself is: what does football want?

'A brand is the reflection of a product or service in the eyes of the general Population', per Kotler (2000). According to Kotler, Filiatrault, and Turner, the brand is intended to differentiate a company's goods or services from the competitor's by creating a word, a sign, a symbol, or a combination of these tools. Solid brands differentiate themselves from competitors by using a unique attribute that makes them special. Additionally, a brand can be identified as a company's promise to its customers. It is also defined as the total emotional experience that a customer has with the products or services of a certain company.

> Branding is the process of researching, developing, and applying a distinctive feature or set of features to your organization so that consumers can begin to associate your brand with your products or services. Branding can be the deciding factor for consumers when they make a purchase decision. Branding gives your business identity beyond its product or service. It gives consumers something to relate to and connect with. Branding makes your business memorable. Branding supports your marketing and advertising efforts. It helps your promotion pack give that extra punch with added recognition and impact. Branding brings your employees pride. When you brand your company, you are giving your business identity and creating a reputable, highly regarded workplace. Strong branding brings in strong employees.
>
> (Allie Decker, 2023)

What is brand identification? It is a strategic analysis to determine a set of statements or ideas used to describe the intended image perceived by a club's supporters (B2C) and customers (B2B) vis-à-vis its competitors.

How exactly is this expressed in football? This involves, for example, the history of the club and which character-determining developments have taken place in the club's history. Think of remarkable moments from the history of the club and the geographical location of the club's home city. Moreover, which iconic players wore the shirt, which historical matches were played, and to what extent was there previous media attention?

## Supporters and fan DNA of a football club

Which products does the club have to offer? Think of the first team, which often functions as the flagship. Moreover, look at the u21 side, the academy, the women's team, the community trust/foundation, and eSports. How do these products relate to each other and other stakeholders, such as the city, the government, and the supporters?

Let us take Liverpool's coach, Jürgen Klopp, as an example. The world-famous motto of this multi-award-winning football club is 'You will never walk alone'. This motto radiates to the entire club, including the fans. This motto is what the entire football club stands for. Because Klopp joined Liverpool in 2015, the playing style of the first team is even better aligned with the identity of the club. The game is aggressive, dynamic, and with high group pressing. The winner's mentality is apparent throughout the club, and the team's togetherness is regularly praised. Together with the fanatically passionate audience closely located to the pitch, this is what the outside world associates with this club.

This did not hold for Pep Guardiola when he became the coach of Bayern Munich in 2013. Guardiola came from FC Barcelona, where he had been very successful with tiki-taka football and was praised worldwide. He did not really succeed in southern Germany, although he was not unsuccessful either. We think this has to do with the stiff structure of the Bayern club, which often has a gruff, surly, and conservative appearance. The club motto, 'Mia san Mia', is roughly translated as 'We do what we want'. This meant that Guardiola was not just walking into the club and that every one of his wishes was granted. The appearance of the brand of the club is fully incorporated into the club structure. Even the passer-by Guardiola could not change this much.

Guardiola left Munich in 2016 for Manchester City, where he contin-ued with what has become his trademark: winning prizes. This success was achieved with beautiful football in Northern England, although the Catalan never equalled the so-called tiki-taka football. Manchester City is now also known for beautiful football, and it fits seamlessly with Pep's conception of the game, which has evolved since his time at FC Barcelona.

Ajax Amsterdam is known for its strong branding of 'For the Future'. The club significantly emphasises its youth academy, which has a long-standing reputation for producing talented players. Football clubs worldwide visit Ajax to learn from their approach to developing young players. The club's goal is to provide opportunities for players to progress to the first team at a young age and showcase their abilities. Although Ajax is not one of the largest clubs in Europe, they recognise that other clubs may acquire their players. This has become a business model for the club, as other teams view the development at Ajax as a valuable trademark. Furthermore, selling players to top clubs generates significant marketing value for the club, making it easier for them to attract top talent to their youth academy. The club's core values are talent, respect, and boldness. These values are integrated into every aspect of the club, both in terms of sports and commercial operations. These values guide their decisions on transfers, sponsorships, and marketing campaigns. On the field, the club demonstrates these values through its renowned youth academy and by giving opportunities to young talented players. They promote a culture of respect on the field, where there are rarely any conflicts or provocations towards the referee or opponents. The team plays an offensive style of football with flair and creativity. Off the field, the club invests in the development of all departments and actively hires and trains non-football talents. The club's campaigns align with its values and are bold and daring but never hurtful or mocking. An example of this is their campaign, where they melted down their Champion trophy and distributed small stars to all their season ticket holders to thank them for their support.

Furthermore, the catchphrase of the Belgian club, Club Brugge KV – 'no sweat, no glory' – suits the club well. Fitting perfectly with the attitude of the supporters and their DNA. Their brand identity was made in collaboration with the fans and has proven crucial in the club's development. Club Brugge KV was surveyed to gather insights from fans on their perceptions of the club's core values. The results revealed that the fans highly valued effort, team spirit, passion, and loyalty. Other values, such as simplicity, essence, and a focus on the sport of soccer, were also identified. Additionally, the survey found that most fans felt a strong connection to the club, with 13% stating that their identity aligns completely with the club's identity and 61% noting a significant overlap. Many fans also reported actively promoting the club to their friends and family (Club Brugge KV, 2011). The club has effectively incorporated these values into its communication and other operations, strengthening the bond with its fanbase and resulting in high demand for season tickets, necessitating a waiting list in 2021.

# Unique selling proposition

One of the most important and difficult decisions that need to be made is the unique selling proposition (USP) of a football club. While every football club has the same products (first team, youth teams, and a football stadium), the football landscape is an extremely dynamic and competitive environment which creates the need for uniqueness. It can be compared with the rivalry between adidas, Nike, Puma, and smaller brands such as Reebok, Under Armour, or New Balance. A few tools can be used to search for a USP for a football club.

DESTEP (a list of categories to list factors that have an impact on your business) links the football club to the country/region/city of origin, with the traditions and character of the people that are following the club. This tool looks at financial resources in the area, the number of companies in the surroundings, the economic situation of inhabitants, and the main club in the city or region.

- **Demographic factors**
  - Local – regional – national – international brand
- **Economic factors**
  - Cost of living – inflation – taxes and duties – finance and credit – working practices – exchange rates – GDP (gross domestic product)
- **Social and cultural factors**
  - Educational level – ethnic identity – religion – lifestyle – customs and values – languages – environmental awareness
- **Technological factors**
  - New products – access to technology – technological lifestyle
- **Ecological factors**
  - Weather – environment – natural resources
- **Political factors**
  - Legal situation – political influences – labour law – trade restrictions – political stability

How do you get all this data and necessary insights before you make any conclusions? A first step could be to collaborate with the city council. They will have a lot of information available on their inhabitants and the economic situation of the country and city. Secondly, data can be collected using social media, tracking your website visitors, and much more. Collaborating with your local or national media could also be very beneficial. They will have a lot of historical data that could be very insightful. Moreover of course, you could always conduct a fan survey.

Take as an example AS Monaco. The brand identity of the football club AS Monaco does not match the DNA of the city of Monaco. When you think about the city of Monaco, you think of Monte Carlo, the nouveau riche, tax haven, fashion, yachts, and Formula 1. These are subjects that are not directly related to the local football club. More foreigners live in Monaco than Monegasques. Because wealthy foreigners cannot identify themselves with the DNA of AS Monaco, the residents are not affiliated with the club. Unfortunately, the club's identity is not linked with fashion, wealth, or luxury. Other football clubs, such as Ajax Amsterdam, Liverpool FC, Real Madrid, and Manchester City, prove that having a strong brand identity matching the DESTEP DNA can have a positive effect to attract more sponsors and more fans.

## Looking for your why

This club's positioning should be open for discussion whenever there are changes or turning points in the football club's life cycle. For example, with the arrival of new owners, expansion to new markets, implementation of a strategic change, or achieving great sporting success for the very first time ever. Thus, the club's management is now ready to turn the brand into a brand story. Let us start by applying the brand to the products of a football club and adding colour to the story of the club's brand.

## Key takeaways

- A strong brand identity differentiates brands from each other.
- Brand identity is something that comes forward from history and actions. It is the personalisation of an enterprise.

- Brand identity is the foundation and DNA of a company, the thing that unites fans.
- Use the DESTEP methodology to define your football club's identity and do not forget to involve your fans.

# References

Club Brugge KV. (2011, January 1). *Club Brugge*. Retrieved from clubbrugge.be: https://www.clubbrugge.be/nl/content/club-fans-lusten-no-sweatno-glory-0

Decker, A. (2023). *The Ultimate Guide to Branding in 2023*. Retrieved from Hubspot: https://blog.hubspot.com/marketing/branding

KAA Gent. (2016, March 12). *KAA Gent*. Retrieved from kaagent.be/nieuws: https://www.kaagent.be/nl/nieuws/12-03-2016/over-het-logo-en-de-bijnaam-van-kaa-gent

Kotler, F. T. (2000). *Le management du marketing*.

Roberts, K. (2004). In K. Roberts, *The Lovemarks Effect*.

# 8 Brand positioning

Have you ever heard about the Golden Circle from Simon Sinek? I will use his theory to help a football club understand how it should determine its brand positioning.

Before integrating the brand positioning into the club's activities, it is crucial for the management or leadership of the football organisation to write down whom you are by using the results from your research during the brand identification exercise of the club. Define your unique brand identity (that makes you stand out from your competitors). Only by undertaking this exercise will you later be able to align your product with its consumers or fans.

To explain how to do this, I would like to use the ideas of Simon Sinek, an English-born American author and motivational speaker. He is the author of five books, including 'Start With Why' and 'The Infinite Game'. Sinek uses the Golden Circle figure below to explain how a brand positioning is chosen.

In his view, and mine, you start with discovering your 'why' (Figure 8.1).

Simon Sinek's Golden Circle is a framework for understanding how successful organisations inspire action. It consists of three elements: Why, How, and What.

For a football club, the Why would be the club's purpose or belief – why they exist and why they do what they do. For example, the club's Why might be to create a sense of community and belonging for fans and to bring people together through a shared love for the game.

The 'How' represents the club's unique approach to achieving its Why. For example, the club's 'How' might be to foster a strong youth academy and promote home-grown talent to the first team.

Finally, the 'What' represents the club's products or services – what the club actually does. For example, the club's 'What' would be playing football matches, organising events, and selling merchandise.

DOI: 10.4324/9781003312680-11

# The Golden Circle

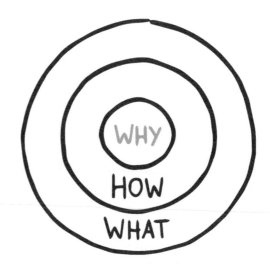

**WHAT**

Every organization on the planet knows WHAT they do. These are products they sell or the services they offer.

**HOW**

Some organizations know HOW they do it. These are the things that make them special or set them apart from their competition.

**WHY**

Very few organizations know WHY they do what they do. WHY is not about making money. That's a result. WHY is a purpose, cause or belief. It's the very reason your organizations exists.

©simonsinek 2022

*Figure 8.1* Simon Sinek's Golden Circle. (With permission from The Optimism Company, 2009, www.simonsinek.com.)

In summary, the Golden Circle is all about understanding the 'why, how, and what' of an organisation and how they are interconnected to inspire others.

When we start with 'Why', we go from the inside to the outside of the circle. 'Why' is the reason to buy, and 'What' merely represents the tangible products as proof of that belief. The 'What' are the reasons we can rationalise why we like a company over another. The 'How' represents a company's strategy to sell its 'What' to achieve its 'Why'.

Let us illustrate this with two non-football examples. You will immediately see why this is so important and that almost no football club has thought this through.

**Coca-Cola**
- **Why:** To spread happiness and refreshment to the world.
- **How:** Creating iconic, delicious, and refreshing beverages brings people together and makes special moments even more enjoyable.
- **What:** By offering a wide range of beverages, including carbonated soft drinks, energy drinks, sports drinks, and water.

**Nike**
- **Why:** To empower athletes everywhere to achieve their full potential.
- **How:** Creating innovative and high-performance products and investing in athlete development and storytelling to inspire and motivate athletes worldwide.
- **What:** By offering a wide range of athletic footwear, apparel, and accessories for various sports and activities.

Now, how does this reflect on football?

**Manchester City FC**
- **Why:** To create a deep, lasting kinship with Manchester communities and cities further afield. A global vision with a focus on local authenticity.
- **How:** Activating participation through the City Football Foundation and the club's dedication to building a sustainable and successful football club.
- **What:** Playing beautiful, attacking football and ensuring the club's sustainability through the City Football Academy.

**Ajax Amsterdam**
- **Why:** To be a club respected and admired for its youth development and innovative approach to the game.
- **How:** Always playing with an attacking and attractive style of football by developing a world-class youth academy and promoting home-grown talent to the first team.
- **What:** Surrounding them with mature and experienced players while also investing in the staff guiding the player's development by giving young talents playing opportunities in the first team.

Nevertheless, such a brand positioning is present in every football club. We never hear owners, board members, staff, players, or other internal stakeholders discuss their 'why'. But should they not? Is it not the best way to convince a partner, fan, or the government to collaborate, follow, or support you by having a clear pathway to your objectives?

For example, I analysed the different steps Manchester City FC took when they changed their badge. The club analysed through a survey how many fans wanted a change of badge, and if they wanted a change, what would that change ideally look like. The three most important symbols for the fans were the Manchester ship, the three rivers, and the red rose. In the end, when the logo was designed, Manchester City FC revealed it with a big show, with logo reveals at the stadium, and even projected on buildings throughout the city.

As far as it has worked at Manchester City FC, there are many examples where a rebranding failed or was less successful. Where Manchester City FC thought about its identity, involving its fans in the new branding, clubs like Everton FC, Leeds United FC, and Cercle Brugge KSV did not. Leeds United FC had to revisit the controversial design of the new badge after a fan back-lash and a petition with over 70.000 signatures. Later, they involved their fans and redesigned their logo (Walters, 2018). Something similar happened to Everton FC, in which the owner changed the crest in 2013 but later had to change it back owing to fan protests (Montgomery, 2013).

To control how the outside world perceives your products, a club needs to strengthen the organisation's mission, vision, and values with personality. Personality is defined by how someone interacts with a brand. This can be divided into four areas: visual, aural, verbal, and behavioural. This explains why all communication channels should align with the positioning and what the look and feel should be. You can compare it to having all the ingredients ready in the kitchen, but it still needs to be cooked and turned into a delicious meal. Most organisations have written this down in a so-called 'brand book'.

For a football club, those ingredients are:

- **Visual:** colours, crest, logos, symbols, pictures, mascot, celebrations
- **Aural:** anthem, chants, music
- **Verbal:** motto, slogan, nicknames, on- and offline communication
- **Behavioural:** all stakeholders, starting with the staff

It is important to have a consistent brand and output and to ensure that qual-ity and credibility are at the forefront of everything you do. Consistency in communication is key to building a strong relationship with consumers and fostering brand loyalty, both among fans and in the club's external environ-ment. While sporting success and emotional impact may be very important, they alone may not be enough to engage people with the football club in the long run.

One of the most important outcomes of building a successful brand is that it leads to the generation of brand equity. Brand equity represents all the benefits a product can achieve with its brand name compared to what would happen if the same product did not have its brand name. 'Brand equity refers to a value premium that a company generates from a product with a recognizable name when compared to a generic equivalent' (Hayes, 2022). It represents the value and quality of a product. An example is when Apple launched the AirPods, a new product for them in an undiscovered market, but because it was an Apple product, people knew it stood for quality and design. Brand equity enables the football club to boost its brand in the eyes of fans and business partners by enhancing perceived quality, raising brand awareness, creating positive associations in the mind of all consumers, and promoting loyalty. A strong identity is necessary when bringing your brand to the market. However, before going to market, knowing who your stakeholders are and what they want would be the next step leading towards a business plan.

## Key takeaways

- Discover the club's 'Why, What, and How' and involve all stakeholders in this exercise.
- Based on the Golden Circle outcome, define the mission, vision, and values of the club.
- The brand representation (visual, aural, verbal, and behavioural) should match each other and with the mission, vision, and values defined for the football club.

## References

Hayes, A. (2022, December 20). *Investopedia*. Retrieved from Brand Equity: https://www.investopedia.com/terms/b/brandequity.asp

Hunter, A. (2013, May 27). *The Guardian/Football*. Retrieved from The Guardian: https://www.theguardian.com/football/2013/may/27/everton-fans-clubs-redesigned-crest

Montgomery, A. (2013, October 3). *designweek*. Retrieved from Design Week: https://www.designweek.co.uk/issues/october-2013/everton-completes-rebrand-reversal-as-fans-choose-new-crest/

The Optimism Company. (2009). START WITH WHY. In S. Sinek, *START WITH WHY* (p. 256). Retrieved from Simon Sinek: http://www.simonsinek.com/

Walters, M. (2018, January 25). *Mirror*. Retrieved from Mirror/sports/football:https://www.mirror.co.uk/sport/football/news/leeds-revisit-controversial-new-badge-11914771

# Customer relationship management

## Simon Van Kerckhoven and Martijn Ernest

Interacting with fans personally allows a football club to communicate its message effectively and at the right time. Once the club has established its brand identity and positioning, it is important to share this with stakeholders. A shared understanding of the club's identity and goals among stakeholders increases the likelihood that they will support and align with its objectives. Access to consumer data is essential for making informed decisions in all commercial aspects of the club. It allows the club to understand and tailor their offerings and approach to different groups of fans.

Fiona Green, an award-winning book writer on data, says: 'Customer relationship management and analysis for sports; the main idea is that getting the right message to the right person at the right time will drive sales. Whether it is increasing participation, demonstrating governance, or improving reputation' (Green, 2021).

This chapter aims to serve as a foundation for understanding the role of CRM in a football club and how it fits within the larger context of the club's brand identity, positioning, legal support, and financial management. It will not provide a detailed guide for implementing CRM in every department but rather it will be used as a starting point for creating a culture of customer-centricity within the club. CRM should not be viewed as a standalone strategy but as an integral part of the club's overall business plan for achieving commercial success. Implementing and integrating it into the club's operations requires significant time, resources, and commitment.

Salesforce has defined CRM as the following:

> Customer relationship management (CRM) is a technology-based approach for managing all your company's relationships and

DOI: 10.4324/9781003312680-12

interactions with customers and potential customers. The goal is simple: improve business relationships.

A CRM system helps companies stay connected to customers, streamline processes, and improve profitability. When people talk about CRM, they usually refer to a CRM system, a tool that helps with contact management, sales management, productivity, and more. A CRM solution helps you focus on your organization's relationships with individual people – including customers, service users, colleagues, or suppliers – throughout your lifecycle with them, including finding new customers, winning their business, and providing support and additional services throughout the relationship.

(Salesforce, 2022)

A CRM system gives everyone – from sales, customer service, business development, recruiting, marketing, or any other line of business – a better way to manage the external interactions and relationships that drive success. A CRM tool lets you store customer and prospect contact information, identify sales opportunities, record service issues, and manage marketing campaigns all in one central location. It makes information about every customer interaction available to anyone at your company who might need it. With visibility and easy access to data, it is easier to collaborate and increase productivity. Everyone in your company can see how customers have been communicated with, what they have bought, when they last purchased, what they paid, and so much more. CRM can help companies of all sizes drive business growth, and it can be especially beneficial to a small business, where teams often need to find ways to do more with less. CRM is not just about software. Data and insight have become the drivers of the successful use of CRM.

## CRM and football

Whether a club has 2,000, 20,000, 200,000, or 2,000,000 fans, they are all individuals with different wants and needs. They expect that the club they support knows who they are. Delivering the right message to the right person at the right time is primarily an issue of knowledge. Only by understanding the customer, their habits, and preferences can the organisation determine what sort of offers a customer will best respond to and identify the moment at which they will be most receptive to them. Football, like any other industry, can or should use CRM. However, five key elements should be in place to make it happen. Only buying the software does not do the trick:

1. **Strategy:** Identification of main goals such as increasing revenue, participation, fan insights, and connecting plus to understand why the club wants to achieve these objectives. What difference will it make to the club's current situation? A club should make a roadmap and highlight the milestones that will help to get from where they are now to where they want to be.
2. **Data:** Data capturing to give the club the foundation to make decisions and personalise messages they want to send to their stakeholders.
3. **Technology:** Ensure the club has the right software and hardware to support the employees implementing this strategy.
4. **Process:** Streamline CRM-related activities throughout the organisation, ensure everybody has access to results, and report these results efficiently.
5. **Culture:** Inter-departmental trust, designated people to support the process, and leadership that believes in this strategy in the long term.

Inter-departmental trust and long-term strategy is the most difficult step for football clubs. To look further into the future without the need for immediate results. For example, Leicester City FC knows what each customer buys, how they interact with the team, what emails they open, what they buy from the team shop, what food products they buy, the types of video games they play, and if they attend home and away matches. This knowledge is available over time and is crucial in the development of commercial objectives.

The ultimate objective when defining a CRM strategy is to:

- Get a 360° overview of every consumer's behaviour
- Improvement of communication tools used to engage with existing consumers
- Identification of new consumers
- Sell out the stadium on matchday
- Sell out activities related to a specific group of consumers on non-matchdays
- Improve commercial revenues such as merchandise, ticketing, food, and drinks

- Offer a better-targeted approach to sponsors
- Creating a culture of collecting data, analysing data, and reporting

# The use of data in football

'CRM databases are essential for clubs to know their customers: therefore, data capture is vitally important to populate the database effectively and ensure a constantly growing record of fans with whom the club would like to develop relationships' (European Club Association, 2018).

'As a club, think of how you can monetize on fandom or engagement. Data can be used to get your consumers to a higher level of engagement with the club: the CRM pyramid' (Green, *Winning with Data*, 2021).

What does the CRM pyramid mean? You will find the passive fan on the bottom layer of the pyramid. Those with a transient interest in a team, a club, or a particular sport but with whom there is no involvement. They are, therefore, unknown to the club. They undoubtedly see themselves as a fan, but there is no contact.

You will find the digitally involved fan on the second layer of the pyramid. They mainly follow the club and club news online and via social media, but there is no interaction with this fan. At this level, they are also unknown because they visit the club's website but do not leave any personal data there yet. Still, if the club would like to, these fans are traceable through their computer's IP address or, for example, their social media identity and accounts such as Facebook or Instagram.

On a higher level, casual fans can be found. They visit a club game at most twice a year, buy something in the fan shop before Christmas, and follow and watch the club's games via an OTT (over-the-top) platform. Their details are known because the club communicates directly with them. Furthermore, because all data and information are collected, the club has enough information to identify these fans personally.

A step above that, frequent fans can be found. They do the same things as casual fans, except they do it more often. Attend more matches during a season, engage more often with the club, and buy more merchandise or other products from the club.

When you arrive at the top of the pyramid, you will find loyal fans there. Those who follow everything, visit as many matches as possible and want to ensure they follow everything their club does. The ultimate objective should

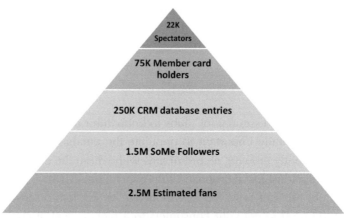

*Figure 9.1* CRM pyramid

be to attract as many loyal fans to your club as possible. To achieve this, a club must let the passive fan take all steps so that he/she eventually becomes a loyal fan. This is attained by collecting the relevant data from the fan, analysing it, and then being involved in a relevant way. During this process, a club must keep trying to get as many new fans into the pyramid's base as possible. Hereunder, you can find an example of a CRM pyramid for a fictional football club (Figure 9.1).

Many clubs today operate as product manager, mainly focusses on how the product can be brought to the consumer. Football clubs should act more as consumer managers. Be more focused on who buys their products, what the consumer wants, and how the club can meet their needs. To this end, all consumer data should be structured in a database management system.

To process all the information, start by focussing on the information you have about an individual, including their contact data. This means you already know who they are, and, subject to their opt-in status, you can communicate with them directly. Go for those direct consumers, those you already interact with, and those you know. Data can be collected through WiFi registration and login, app registration and login, purchase of merchandising through the web shop, email program, website registration, and log in.

It is important that, ultimately, everyone can be found in the database. The supporters who buy tickets for the match, the members of the fan club, the corporate clients, online clients, volunteers, and even the players and referees.

The importance of demographic data cannot be underestimated. This means knowing the age, gender, education, income, profession, civil, and family situation. However, even more important than this is the behavioural data. This information tells the football club how stakeholders interact with the club, both online and offline. Do they attend organised events? Or visit the website? Furthermore, if so, what do they read or view? Have they downloaded the club app, and are they visiting the social media channels?

# Single customer view

A single customer view is an aggregation of all an organisation's data on a particular customer, presented to give a clear overview of each customer and their specific data. In other words, it allows you to create a profile of your customer so you can get a clear overview of where they are at in regard to your business.

(Boyd, 2018)

There are different data points a football club would like to collect to get a long-term commercial advantage. These data points are necessary to reach a complete single customer view (SCV). This means having a profile for each customer in which you can analyse their previous ticketing purchase history, attendance history, which food and beverages they bought when attending a match, if they bought merchandise previously, whether they are active online and connected to the club's social media channels, if they participate in contests, and what is their household situation.

Club membership are among the best ways to get to know your direct consumers. Why? Although there are multiple points from where you can collect data, you probably need to start with the fans who are already high up the CRM pyramid because they already agreed to hand over their data to the club. The most complete and ideal data collection touchpoint is when a consumer decides to join the club. Although clubs approach the design of a membership scheme differently as shown in the table hereunder (Table 9.1).

Memberships have traditionally been seen as generating more income (paying to join and getting some benefits that other fans do not have). In some countries, there are other examples where the legal form of club membership is mandatory. In Germany, there is the well-known 50+1 rule.

The 50+1 rule is a regulation in German football that requires clubs to hold most of their voting rights. This means that at least 51% of a club's

Table 9.1 Football Club Membership Packages

| Liverpool FC | • Ticketing focussed program<br>• Access to tickets<br>• Junior proposition (retail) | CR Vasco da Gama | • Ticketing focussed program<br>• Discount on tickets<br>• National retail network |
|---|---|---|---|
| FC Barcelona | • Membership as a closed community<br>• Fans vote on President<br>• Status reward | SL Benfica | • National retail network<br>• Benefits in many sports & schools<br>• Ticketing benefits |
| Real Madrid | • Membership as a closed community<br>• Fans vote on President<br>• Membership tiering for internationals | NYCFC | • Season ticket proposition<br>• Driving sales<br>• Experiential |

voting rights must be held by its members rather than by outside investors or companies. The rule is intended to prevent outside investors from gaining too much control over the club and ensure that it remains firmly rooted in its community. The rule is used in the Bundesliga and the 2. Bundesliga. The members of a German football club who hold a majority of the voting rights under the 50+1 rule have the right to vote on important decisions related to the club, such as the election of board members, the approval of financial reports, and changes to the club's bylaws. They also have the right to participate in general meetings to discuss and vote on proposals put forward by the club's board of directors. Other elements often used to add value to a membership program include prioritising ticket sales at discounted prices and access to exclusive merchandise and events.

However, in many cases, data collection is only sometimes linked to memberships. The membership card reinforces the feeling of belonging, which fans/consumers give easy access to their data. This can also be extended. Let us take a closer look at the example of ACF Fiorentina. The Italian club launched the fan card Viola Pride in 2010, a collaboration between the club and local institutions, to actively involve fans in and encourage their involvement. The city of Florence was an ideal environment for this owing to multiple commercial opportunities. The rechargeable smart card contained the demographic information of the individual fan and could be used for various online and offline purchases in addition to buying match tickets (Chanavat, 2019).

Four years later, in 2014, the possibilities of the card were further expanded, and the name changed to the 'InViola' card. This also made it an ultimate tool within relationship marketing. More than 70,000 fans of Fiorentina were allowed to participate and take advantage of countless extras, such as personally signed shirts, a stadium tour, or even participation in a training camp of the club. Additionally, the card can also be used at companies that sponsor the club. Incidentally, the card could not be used as a means of payment on the recommendation of fan clubs, as this could imply economic exploitation. This smart card offers an excellent opportunity for Fiorentina to collect more information about the fans. Upon receiving additional data from its fans, AFC Fiorentina should be able to, over time, collect and archive information on its direct consumers. Asking someone directly to give you their information will result in the most accurate data if it results in value exchange (a membership card does). Linking the data collection to their membership or fan cards enables them to trace and qualify consumers.

Something AS Saint-Etienne (ASSE) did:

In its ambition to create the largest community of fans in France, the club introduced its 'ASSE member card'. Through this card, the fans have an account on the official website and their points are assigned to each of their purchases in the club's profit centres. They also enjoy discounts and can participate in events and experience unique moments within the club. The project was launched in 2014, and only 12 months later, 18,000 members signed up. This data was collected in a database, ensuring a better understanding of the needs of the fans could be put in place. Showing that CRM's goal is not to collect information but to treat and analyse it in depth. A success story on how a member card was created to understand the members' buying habits and thus to meet their needs and offer them personalised offers (AS Saint-Etienne, sd).

Nowadays, you will often see the integration of NFTs and/or Fan Tokens in addition to or as a replacement for the membership card. This will be discussed further later in chapter 21, 'Business Development'.

The main data you would like to receive is the so-called 'first-party' data. The data the club collected itself and not through third parties. This data should contain individual contact information, demographical information such as age, gender, education, and income level, behavioural data (event attendance, open email rate, online engagement), and transactional information such as payments and event-related data. Important as well is to learn more about the needs of the customer. What is their expectation of the football club? Which products are interesting for them? The last category of data you want to collect is lifestyle data which are the elements of interest to the club's sponsors or different interests outside the club, such as hobbies. This way, we create a complete overview of a fan, the SCV.

Besides SCV, there are two database definitions that we still need to discuss. The first is DMP (Data Management Platform) and CDP (Customer Data Platform). What are the main differences? A DMP manages all the data of your customers who are a little lower in the CRM pyramid compared to the SCV. You can reach them through a digital IP or cookie, but you have no further information. A CDP often refers to the database environment that brings both data sets together.

## Consumer segmentation

Obtained all your data and allocated it to a data management system (DMP)? Do you have your SCV in place? Perfect! Then now, it is time to figure out who your consumers and fans really are. Cosmetically manufacturing your ideal customers based on the data you have in your SCV, DMP, or CDP. This can be done in three stages through three questions:

- **Geographical spread:** Where do my fans come from?
- **Data standardisation:** Which of my fans share similar habits or have similar needs?
- **Customer personas:** What is the ideal fan per segmented group?

## Geographical spread

Where are my fans located? It is important to know which products you can offer your fans, how they travel to the stadium on matchday, and their interaction with the club. For example, a fan located 200 kilometres away from the stadium can probably not attend open training every week. Nevertheless, if this fan works in the neighbourhood of the training facilities, they can view a training during their lunch time or have business meetings while sitting next to the pitches.

Below is an example of the geographical spread of four clubs in Belgium: Standard de Liège, KV Kortrijk, KAA Gent, and KRC Genk. The main conclusion is that Standard de Liège has a national fanbase from all different

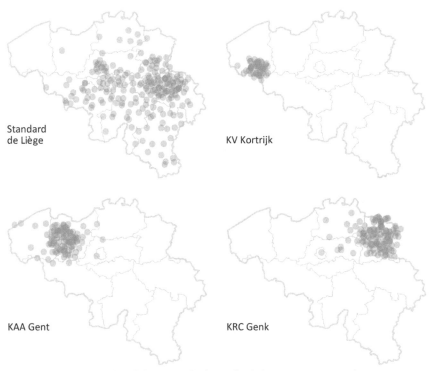

*Figure 9.2* Geographical fan spread of Standard de Liège, KV Kortrijk, KAA Gent, and KRC Genk

regions in Belgium. Football clubs like KRC Genk and KAA Gent have a more provincial fanbase where the fans mainly live in the province where the club is located. At a smaller club like KV Kortrijk, we can see that the fanbase is local in and around the city of Kortrijk (Figure 9.2).

# Data standardisation

Two examples of similar habits that can be used to put certain consumers in one group and, further down the road, create a customer persona of this group by looking into their behaviour before, during, and after the match. Through a survey, you can identify if a fan attends the fan entertainment zone, if they have a meeting point to meet with friends whether they enter the fan shop before the game. This will give a better understanding of your fans and help in the decision-making process of fan engagement activities.

# Customer personas

'These buyer personas are research-based archetypal modelled representations of who your fans are, what they are trying to accomplish, which goals drive their behaviour, how they think, what they buy, and why they make buying decisions' (Zambito, 2013).

Traditionally, they are divided into B2C (fans whose consumption is strictly transactional. They buy standardised football products such as season tickets, single tickets, basic food and beverages, merchandising, and participate in other matchday-related events) and B2B consumers (sponsors, partners and match day and non-matchday-related events with a focus on enhancing business opportunities).

The Belgian football club KRC Genk has created four categories with multiple subcategories to categorise their fans. These categories are:

1. Freaks (those that are emotionally attached to sportive results)
2. Geeks (the ones that have a statistical mindset and care about data and facts)
3. Normies (families and normal – regular fans)
4. Business
   - Selfie (fans that attend games only for the glitter and glamour)
   - Farmer (attend games to network and meet new people)
   - Hunter (trying to do business on matchdays and sell their products/services)
   - Partners (sponsors of the club bringing clients for entertainment)

Each football club can decide how they categorise their fans based on the club's needs, infrastructure, and goals. What is more important is what you do next after the club has completed the segmentation of its fans.

# Fan engagement

Customer knowledge is of little value without the means to act on it. Once you know who your consumers are, you will be able to find a way to communicate the club's values to all stakeholders, in the right way, at the right time. This is what often is referred to as fan engagement.

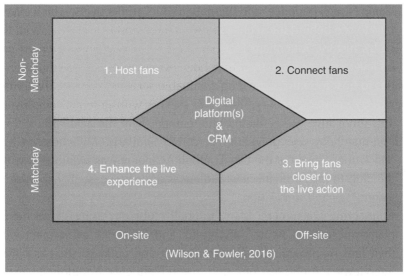

*Figure 9.3* Fan engagement model (see Geoff Wilson & David Fowler, 2016)

What is fan engagement?

A growth strategy of long-term relationship management between sports institutions and fan groups, where institutions facilitate fans in self-expression and in-group acceptance, using modern online and offline technologies, to create social value for fans, which can be transformed into profit optimization.

(Schnater, 2016)

As fan engagement became a buzzword in the football industry over the last couple of years, it got heavily misused, focussing on all activities organised by a sports entity. Fan experience is part of a fan engagement strategy; providing an experience to a consumer is part of the strategy to engage a consumer. In short, setting up inflatables in front of your stadium has little to do with engaging consumers. Consumer engagement is more than one activation; it is more than just optimising the welfare of fans. It is a strategy with the following structure (Figure 9.3).

Geoff Wilson explains their fan engagement model as follows:

1. **Hosting fans:** Football clubs such as FC Barcelona and Real Madrid already host several events and activities for fans, such as the 'Spotify

Camp Nou Experience' and 'Bernabéu Tour', respectively, which allows fans to see behind the scenes of the stadium and learn more about the club's history. Tottenham Hotspur showcased how sports venues can be leveraged for more than matchday events. They utilised their facilities to host job fairs, providing a valuable service to the local community by connecting over 3,000 job seekers with potential employers. This innovative use of their venue earned them the accolade of 'best non-matchday use of venue' in 2015. Similarly, Manchester City's 'Hackathon' event at the City Football Academy was a unique way for the club to engage with new audiences and showcase its expertise in technology and innovation.

2. **Connecting consumers:** Many football clubs are using social media platforms such as Twitter, Instagram, and Facebook to connect with their fans by providing exclusive content and updates, such as player interviews, training sessions, and match highlights. Additionally, many clubs use messaging apps such as WhatsApp and Telegram to create fan groups to communicate directly with fans. An example of fan engagement through connection is Liverpool FC's collaboration with Skype. The platform lets the club to connect with fans and create a direct communication channel through its official Skype account. Furthermore, new technologies such as virtual reality, augmented reality, and 360-degree video are becoming more popular among sports clubs; they can create immersive experiences that give fans a glimpse of what happens behind the scenes.

3. **Bringing consumers closer to the live action:** Football clubs increasingly use live streaming and OTT platforms such as Amazon Prime, Facebook Live, and YouTube to broadcast their matches to fans who cannot attend the stadium. Clubs also invest in virtual reality and augmented reality technology to create immersive matchday experiences for fans.

4. **Enhancing the live experience:** Football clubs like Manchester United and Bayern Munich have already started to enhance the live experience for fans by incorporating interactive elements and experiences such as virtual reality, augmented reality, and mobile apps that provide real-time match statistics and updates. Clubs are also investing in creating fan zones, such as the Manchester City square, and providing various food and merchandise options for the fans inside the stadium.

The Real Madrid app illustrates how a sports club can utilise technology to achieve multiple goals. It includes features such as replay options from different angles for fans at the stadium, which enhances the live experience, real-time match statistics, and a tunnel cam, which brings fans closer to the live action, a feature for fans to create their profile, which helps them connect with other fans, and access to the Real Madrid store, which allows fans to purchase merchandise. As sports clubs focus on growing their business through CRM, choosing platforms becomes increasingly important (Wilson, 2016).

It is not easy to go from a matchday to everyday engagement, but hopefully, we have given you some food for thought to bring your consumers closer to your club and reduce your reliance on the matchday experience.

## Consumer development framework

Putting people first can only be done if you know what they are doing; so, for every activity that a club organises, you should make up a customer pathway. This is crucial in optimising the service and shows in detail how B2C and B2B actors consume your brand. It helps optimise service, builds a culture of checking quality, ensures data collection in every club operation, and guides future employees.

The eventual goal of a consumer framework is to use this culture of CRM and customer engagement to develop a strategy in every club department that puts the consumer first. Resulting in an easier job for the commercial staff to turn data into consumption.

## Key takeaways

- Data is the new gold; a CRM structure and strategy are crucial in each football club.
- Make sure there are multiple data collection points and list which data you want to collect from the fans.
- Work towards the creation of an SCV to have a 360-degree profile of each fan.
- Segmentation of fans in different groups based on the collected data.
- Create a fan engagement strategy for every segmentation group.
- Implement the CRM culture in every department and work towards a personalised consumer experience.

# References

AS Saint-Etienne. (sd). *Devenir Membre*. Retrieved from upporter.asse.fr: https://supporter.asse.fr/?_ga=2.56010219.158092207.1674577227-1850141590.1674577227

Boyd, J. (2018, Augustus 2). *Single Customer View*. Retrieved from Brandwatch: https://www.brandwatch.com/blog/single-customer-view/

Chanavat, N. (2019). Routledge Handbook of Football Marketing. In N. Chavanat, *Handbook of Football Marketing* (pp. 351–368). Taylor & Francis.

European Club Association. (2018). In *Club Management Guide*.

Geoff, W. & D. Fowler. (2016). Fan Engagement Model.

Green, F. (2021). In *Winning with Data*. Taylor & Francis.

Green, F. (2021). Winning with Data. In F. Green, *Winning with Data* (p. 244). Taylor & Francis.

Salesforce. (2022, August 10). *Salesforce/What Is a crm*. Retrieved from: https://www.salesforce.org/blog/what-is-a-crm/

Schnater, B. (2016). *Defining Fan Engagement*. LinkedIn.

Wilson, G. (2016, September 23). Fan Engagement: From Match Day to Every Day. Retrieved from: https://www.linkedin.com/pulse/fan-engagement-from-match-day-every-geoff-wilson/

Zambito, T. (2013). *What Is a Buyer Persona*. Retrieved from tonyzambito.com: https://tonyzambito.com/about/what-is-a-buyer-persona/

# 10 Legal support and regulations

Simon Van Kerckhoven and
Martijn Ernest

As regulations continue to increase, obtaining legal advice has become increasingly paramount. The globalisation of football has transformed the sport into a multifaceted industry with diverse stakeholders and competing interests. Football clubs need to have a knowledgeable lawyer familiar with a wide range of legal topics to protect these interests. Ensuring that the club's employees, players, sponsors, and fans are fully legally protected is paramount.

Not all football clubs have an in-house counsel, and some work closely with local legal firms to handle legal disputes. However, when a club is actively transferring players, having at least one in-house lawyer with knowledge of player contracts, commercial, and employment contracts is recommended. As the club's activities expand, integrating additional legal departments may be necessary. Additionally, working with a local legal firm can bring diverse expertise, experience, and resources.

Preventing problems is more effective than mitigating damages. With that in mind, this overview aims to provide insight into the legal tasks that football clubs need to address, primarily from a commercial perspective.

There is no such thing as a football law. Although there are numerous examples of 'the law' treating sporting activities, sporting bodies, and the resolution of disputes in sports differently from other activities and bodies, a clear difference needs to be made between law and regulations:

DOI: 10.4324/9781003312680-13

# Law

Public face of football law

> refers to the influence of nation-state governments, parliaments, and courts on football and the activities of international organisations such as the European Union, and the Council of Europe. The football-related legislation, jurisprudence, and activity of these bodies generate national, EU and international law respectively.
>
> (Parrish & Pedlebury, 2019)

For example: The European Commission and Nike in 2019:

(European Commission, 2019)

On 25 March 2019, the European Commission fined Nike €12.5 million for banning traders from selling licensed merchandise to other countries within the European Economic Area (EEA). This restriction concerned merchandising products of some of Europe's best-known football clubs and federations, for which Nike held the licence. The EU Commission investigation found that Nike's non-exclusive licensing and distribution agreements breached EU (European Union) competition rules:

1. Nike imposed several direct measures restricting out-of-territory sales by licensees, such as clauses prohibiting these sales, obligations to refer orders for out-of-territory sales to Nike, and clauses imposing double royalties for out-of-territory sales.
2. Nike enforced indirect measures to implement the out-of-territory restrictions, for instance, threatening licensees with ending their contract if they sold out-of-territory, refusing to supply 'official product' holograms if it feared that sales could be going towards other territories in the EEA, and carrying out audits to ensure compliance with the restrictions.
3. In some cases, Nike used master licensees in each territory to grant sub-licences for using the different IPRs (Intellectual Property Rights) to third parties. To secure the practice through the whole distribution chain, Nike imposed direct and indirect measures on master licensees. Through these measures, Nike compelled master licensees to stay within their territories and to enforce restrictions vis-à-vis their sub-licensees.
4. Nike included clauses that explicitly prohibited licensees from supplying merchandising products to customers, often retailers, who could sell

outside the allocated territories. In addition to obliging licensees to pass on these prohibitions in their contracts, Nike would ensure that retailers (e.g. fashion shops and supermarkets) stopped purchasing products from licensees in other EEAs.

The EU Commission has concluded that Nike's illegal practices, which were in force for approximately 13 years (from 1 July 2004 until 27 October 2017), partitioned the single market and prevented licensees in Europe from selling products cross-border, to the ultimate detriment of European consumers. Nike's illegal practices affected to varying degrees the licensed merchandise products bearing the brands of clubs like FC Barcelona, Manchester United, Juventus, Inter Milan, and AS Roma, and national federations like the French Football Federation. Regarding the level of the fine, the EU Commission considered the value of sales relating to the infringement, the gravity of the infringement, and its duration, and the fact that Nike cooperated with the EU Commission during the investigation. The fine imposed by the EU Commission on Nike amounts to €12,555,000.

# Regulations

Private face of football law:

> refers to the statutes and regulations of the competent football authorities and the jurisprudence of the various dispute resolution bodies operating at domestic (national associations and national courts of arbitration for sports), continental (UEFA and its equivalents; AFC, CONMEBOL, CAF, OFC & CONCACAF) and global (FIFA and Court of Arbitration for Sport) levels.
>
> (Parrish & Pedlebury, 2019)

An example of such disciplinary regulations would be the following: (UEFA, 2019)

These regulations contain the substantive and formal provisions governing the punishment of any breach of UEFA's statutes, regulations, directives, or decisions, apart from any breach of the UEFA Club Licensing and Financial Fair Play Regulations. The following list of disciplinary measures may be considered by the relevant disciplinary body when rendering its decision (Table 10.1).

Table 10.1 UEFA Disciplinary Regulations (Courtesy of UEFA, 2019)

| UEFA disciplinary regulations | | |
|---|---|---|
| **Offence type** | **First offence** | **Second offence** |
| Invasion of the field of play | €5K fine | €8K fine |
| Lighting of fireworks | No. of fireworks x €500 | No. of fireworks x €500 + 50% |
| Use of laser pointer or similar | €8K fine | €12K fine |
| Message not fit for a sports event | 10K fine | €15K fine |
| Act of damage | €5K fine + damages | €8K fine + damages |
| Late kick-off | Warning (coach & team) | €10K fine + 1 match under probation (coach) |

Understanding the difference between national/international law and regulations set by footballing bodies is key to knowing the functioning of the legal department in a club or the assignments that need to be outsourced to a legal firm.

Various areas of law applicable to the activities of almost any professional football club:

- **Sports law:** Transfer contracts, employment agreements with players, disciplinary matters, interpretation of regulations, transfer agreements, training compensation, and solidarity mechanisms
- **Civil law:** Commercial agreements, HR, debt collection, …
- **Corporate law:** Statutory affairs and corporate governance
- **Administrative law:** Construction permits, insurance, and tax issues
- **Intellectual property law:** Registration and protection of copyrights and trademarks

Apart from the areas of law, the legal counsel's task at football clubs focus on two main objectives: (European Club Association, 2018)

Legal risk mitigation: Identifying and minimising legal risks

- Reviewing and drafting transfer/employment agreements, including bank guarantees, compliance with football regulations, and jurisdiction clauses.
- Reviewing and drafting commercial agreements, including due diligence in business transactions and non-compete clauses in sponsorship agreements.
- Providing guidance to the board in strategic decision-making.

- Ensuring compliance with labour laws.
- Ensuring compliance with sports-related regulations, such as anti-doping and fan conduct regulations.
- Protecting intellectual property rights.

**Legal support services:**

1. Establishing standardised protocols and agreements.
2. Maintaining a centralised legal database for club departments.
3. Ensuring data privacy compliance.
4. Providing standard employment and commercial agreements.
5. Conducting background checks on partners and stakeholders.
6. Advising on the club's organisational structure.

# Impact on the club's operational services

Enough theory. We want to avoid turning you into a lawyer or legal counsel. However, as a general manager, commercial manager, or marketer, you must understand the legal implications when operating a club or striking a commercial deal. We do not give a complete overview of how law/legislation/regulation impacts the club's operation services but focus on data protection/General Data Protection Regulation (GDPR), image rights, and potential fines.

# Data protection/GDPR

Engaging with your fans on a non-matchday is crucial. The close attachment and emotional connection fans have with their football club makes them interesting for sponsors to get in touch with. After establishing a Customer Relationship Management culture at the club, the club has the tools to reach anyone with any message at any time. But can a football club sell such services to everyone? Can a football club store data and use it in the way that suits them best? And most importantly, can they use your data to help their sponsors and partners?

On 25 May 2018, the EU set out a game-changing data privacy law, GDPR. Sam Galtis explained GDPR as the following:

General Data Protection Regulation is, simply put, a long list of regulations for handling consumer data. This new legislation aims to help align existing data protection protocols while increasing the levels of protection for individuals. The end goal is to help customers gain a greater level of control over their data, while offering more transparency throughout the data collection and use processes. These new laws will help to bring existing legislation up to par with the connected digital age we live in. Since data collection is such a normal and integral aspect of our personal and business lives, it helps set the standard for data-related laws moving forward. GDPR is a regulation that you will want to take seriously.

(Saltis, GDPR Explained, 2020)

Fiona Green explains in her book, *Winning with Data*, GDPR in football (Green, 2021):

In the football industry, it is crucial to comply with the GDPR when handling personal data. The GDPR is a comprehensive data protection law that guarantees individuals certain rights with regard to their personal data.

Football clubs must respect the rights of all individuals whose data is stored in their systems, whether they are fans, ticket buyers, customers, players, coaches, referees, volunteers, staff members, or sponsors. These individuals have the right to information disclosure, access, correction, and restriction of processing.

Information disclosure refers to how personal data is used and processed, including communication, profiling, and decision-making. For example, if a club wants to use personal data to send marketing emails, they must obtain the individual's consent and provide clear information on how their data will be used. Similarly, if a club plans to use personal data to analyse fan behaviour, they must inform the individual of their intention and obtain their consent.

Access refers to giving individuals access to their personal data, including confirmation that their information is being processed and any other supplementary information the club may have about them. For instance, if a club stores personal data of its fans, it should allow them to access their data and review it. This could include their name, email address, and purchase history.

Correction provides individuals with the opportunity to correct any inaccurate or incomplete information the club has about them. For example, if a club has misspelled a fan's name or has an outdated email address, the fan has the right to request a correction.

Finally, individuals have the right to request the restriction of processing, which means that the club cannot further process their personal data, although the club can still retain the existing information it has. For instance, if a fan unsubscribes from receiving the club's emails, the club cannot send any further marketing emails, but they can still retain the fan's information for their internal records.

## Case of Leicester City Football Club's online security breach: (Leicester City Football Club, 2019)

The club discovered a criminal online security breach, which had compromised the personal and financial information of some users of its online retail platform between 23 April and 4 May 2019. All supporters potentially affected were immediately identified and contacted to alert them to the breach and to recommend appropriate action. Upon discovering the breach, the security of their retail platform was immediately restored, and appropriate measures were taken to ensure the security of all other online assets. In line with its GDPR responsibilities, the club informed all necessary parties – including potentially affected users, the police, and the Information Commissioners Office (ICO) – and launched an immediate investigation into the source of the breach. The club has been in direct contact with all users potentially affected by this breach and used this crisis to update their consumer data and allow consumers to update their data status by providing a link to a personal information form on their website.

## Image rights

Image rights in football refer to the commercial use of a player's name, likeness, and other personal attributes for marketing and promotional purposes. This includes the use of a player's image for merchandise, advertising, sponsorships, and endorsements.

Image rights are separate from a player's standard employment contract and are often negotiated separately. They are usually owned by the player and can be licensed to third parties for a fee. In some cases, image rights are also held by the club, and the player may receive a percentage of the revenue generated from their use.

The value of image rights in football is significant, particularly for high-profile players. Clubs can use the likeness of star players to generate revenue through merchandise sales and sponsorships, while players can earn additional income through image rights deals.

To protect image rights, players and clubs may enter into contracts that specify how a player's image can be used and by whom. This can include restrictions on the use of their image by competitors or in certain types of advertising. Players may also appoint agents or lawyers to negotiate image rights deals on their behalf.

In some cases, disputes can arise over image rights. For example, a player may object to the use of their image in a particular way or by a particular company, or a club may claim ownership of a player's image rights. In such cases, legal action may be required to resolve the dispute.

Esteve Calzada identifies in his book 'Show Me The Money' three types of players' image rights that can be sold by marketers (Calzada, 2013).

In the world of football, image rights play a critical role in commercialisation, and they are classified into three distinct categories: Group official rights, individual official image rights, and personal image rights.

Group official rights involve the use of a group of players' images wearing their team's official clothing. Such rights are typically obtained through players' contracts of employment or participation, which allows the club or national side to use and commercially exploit the group image. For instance, an ad campaign featuring Manchester United players wearing the team's official jersey for a Teamviewer promotion.

Individual official image rights refer to a single player's right to commercialise their image while wearing official team clothing. The player needs a specific agreement with the team to exploit their image commercially. Moreover, the team cannot use the player's image, even when dressed in club clothing, without their permission. Many teams include clauses in their players' contracts to define the situations in which they can use the individual player's official image rights, which are often offered to the team's official sponsors. For example, Nike's campaign featuring Mbappé wearing a PSG kit.

Personal image rights refer to a player's image when not wearing official clothing or using products featuring sports properties' distinguished symbols. These rights are owned by the players, giving them complete control over how their image is used commercially. For instance, a campaign featuring Lionel Messi promoting a sports drink while not wearing any team clothing.

Football players, teams, and sponsors need to comprehend these different types of image rights to navigate the complex landscape of commercialisation in the football industry. Properly managing and negotiating these rights can help stakeholders maximise the value of their commercial partnerships while avoiding disputes over unauthorised use or exploitation of players' images.

## Case of Mohammed Salah and the Egyptian FA: (Cohen, Lawinsport, 2019)

The unauthorised use of the image of Liverpool star and Egyptian international Mohammed Salah by the Egyptian Football Association (EFA) in April 2018 sparked a high-profile legal dispute, drawing attention to the importance of international players' image rights. Salah has licensed his image rights to two companies, one of which, MS Commercial (Cayman), is directed by his lawyer and representative. Salah's image rights companies likely have separate agreements with Liverpool FC and adidas, allowing the use of his image in a 'club context' and a 'personal context', respectively. However, the EFA had not established any image rights agreements with Salah or the Egyptian team. This led to a dispute between Salah, his image rights companies, and the EFA, as the EFA allegedly used Salah's image without authorisation to endorse a competitor of one of Salah's endorsement deals with Vodafone. The incident created problems for all parties involved.

## Potential fines

Fines are a common disciplinary measure used by governing bodies in football, such as National Associations, National Leagues, and UEFA, to deal with clubs that have violated regulations. While this cost may not be universally applicable to all clubs, it may be more significant to some clubs than others. In specific cases, fines represent a sizeable percentage of the overall club budget. This can be particularly challenging for smaller clubs with limited financial resources.

Fines are never a good thing, as they represent a form of punishment and can negatively impact a club's reputation and finances. Governing bodies may impose football-specific fines for poor disciplinary performance or specific incidents that may have happened on or off the pitch during a match, such as a security breach or player brawl. These fines can range from minor monetary penalties to hefty fines or even points deductions, depending on the severity of the violation.

Given the reactionary nature of fines, planning for them in advance is usually impossible, especially from a budgeting point of view. However, a degree of contingency planning may be possible, and certainly advisable in the case of suspended fines that certain actions or behaviours could trigger. This could include setting aside funds to cover potential fines or implementing policies and procedures to prevent potential violations. Being proactive and minimising the risk of fines, clubs can better protect their finances and reputation.

## Case of Legia Warszawa SA

The best atmosphere I have ever experienced in a stadium was during my visit to Warsaw with chants, fireworks, pyro, banners, flags, and tifos. The club portrays itself as fierce, dynamic, and tough. And so are their fans, and their ultras; maybe not the ones you would want to be close friends with, but they know how to stir things up in a non-violent way. Yet, this is not always well received by the Polish football authorities. The club knows that a more extreme form of support is inherent to how their fans show their passion for the club. From a marketing and sporting point of view (note: that I do not promote violence or any illegalities to take place), a passionate following is an absolute advantage. However, from a financial/legal point of view, it is a risk. In 2017, UEFA fined the club for their supporters displaying a political banner commemorating the Warsaw Uprising in 1944 before a Champions League qualifying game. The result? A 35,000 EURO fine for a banner is pretty heavy. The fans did not accept this without providing UEFA with an answer; they reacted with another banner portraying the UEFA logo with a pig in the middle and the sub-text 'And the 35,000 EURO fine goes to…'. What is the club's reaction to these kinds of incidents? Allocate funds when making up a budget to cover potential fines so that these fines will not severely impact the club's financial situation. It is a much better solution than trying to change the DNA of the club.

Many areas of law reflect on what is often called football law. To understand the different areas that apply to football, you need specialists. Large clubs or organisations will need different profiles with different legal backgrounds. Smaller football clubs or organisations can best hire an external law firm so the club can rely on its expertise. This differs from the situation in chapter 11, "Financial Management." As a football club, you better have a financial expert, and it better be very good one.

## Key takeaways

- Football has become big business and therefore the influence of lawyers has only increased ever since. Having an expert in-house to check all legal contracts and implications is crucial.
- Knowing the regulations and potential fines from UEFA and the domestic league can prevent financial surprises during the season.
- Image rights of top football players have become incredibly valuable and necessary for football clubs to hold those rights for sponsor contracts.
- GDPR is very important for a club collecting data from its fans.

## References

Calzada, E. (2013). In E. Calzada (Ed.), *Show Me the Money!* Bloomsbury.

Cohen, J. (2019, April 09). *Lawinsport*. Retrieved from Lawinsport.com: https://www.lawinsport.com/topics/sports/item/image-rights-and-international-footballers-the-curious-case-of-mohamed-salah-and-the-egypt-football-association?category_id=152

European Club Association. (2018). *In Club Management Guide*. ECA.

European Commission. (2019). *Antitrust Nike Press Release*. Commissioner Margrethe Vestager.

Green, F. (2021). *Winning with Data*. Taylor & Francis.

Leicester City Football Club. (2019, June 1). *Club Statement*. Retrieved from Lcfc.com: https://www.lcfc.com/news/1232342/club-statement-online-security-breach/press-release

Mark & Clerk. (2016, February 25). *Lexology*. Retrieved from https://www.lexology.com/library/detail.aspx?g=acc49cc6-66e1-49b7-a142-854b00333a37

Parrish & Pedlebury. (2019). Football Law. In Richard Parrish & Adam Pendlebury (Eds.), *Routledge Football Business and Management* (pp. 71–72). Taylor & Francis.

Saltis, S. (2020, December 07). GDPR Explained.

UEFA. (2019). *Disciplinary Regulations*. UEFA.

# Financial management

## Simon Van Kerckhoven and Martijn Ernest

Football clubs and good financial management, it is something that, on numerous occasions, does not go hand in hand. Unfortunately, football clubs became a trophy asset for many investors to show off and feed their egos. The number of articles in the newspapers announcing football clubs making millions and millions of debt or even football clubs going bankrupt owing to financial mismanagement are countless. While reading this, you can come up with many examples from your favourite league. Finance might not be the sexiest topic to cover, but it is one of the most important ones. Therefore, I describe this as one of the five building blocks to leading a football club to commercial success.

Football clubs are businesses; that is clear. However, it would be completely blunt to reality if I said that common business and financial principles could be transferred to the football industry. Yes, football clubs have, like other businesses, a certain level of financial accountability whereby financial reporting is an essential element to measure the level of club management and oversee the overall economic state of a club. Moreover a financial benchmark to other businesses or actors in the overall entertainment industry can help assess the football club's health find a compromise between available resources and overall ambitions. However, the big difference is that football has its economic and financial peculiarities.

The 2013 UEFA Club Licensing Benchmark report provides insights into the financial performances of clubs throughout Europe; 63% of Europe's top-division clubs reported operating losses, 38% of its clubs were in negative equity positions (liabilities exceeding assets), and auditors expressed serious concern as to the validity of the 'going concern assumptions' at one

DOI: 10.4324/9781003312680-14

in seven clubs (Morrow, 2017a). In the 2020 edition of this report, disclosing insights from the financial year 2018, UEFA sees a positive evolution;

> The 2018 financial year was the second consecutive year of overall profitability for European top division club football – a significant turnaround compared with the €5bn of losses that were recorded in just three years at the turn of the decade. Just as important for the underlying health of football is the continued strengthening of club balance sheets, with clubs' assets exceeding their liabilities/debts by €9bn at the end of 2018.
>
> (UEFA, 2020a)

Despite this positive trend, there are still some pressing issues in terms of football finance – this is what we like to understand in the particular football situation.

The biggest challenge for clubs is finding the right balance between operating income and their biggest cost, the wages of the players and sporting staff. UEFA explains the situation as follows:

> Wages increased in 17 of the top 20 leagues, with only Austria, the Netherlands, and Greece reporting a decrease in wages, albeit a marginal decrease for the first two. In local currency percentage terms, Turkey posted the highest wage growth of 36% (6% in Euro terms) owing to the sharp depreciation of the lira against the euro and the payment of part of their wage bill in the US dollar or EURO. Germany has the lowest wage-to-revenue ratio (53%) in the top 20 leagues. At the other end of the scale, France, Russia, Turkey, Portugal, Belgium, Switzerland, Ukraine, Greece, Israel, and Poland have average wage bills of between 70% and 80% of their revenue. Given that other – mainly fixed – operating costs tend to consume between 33% and 40% of revenues, a wage-to-revenue ratio over 70% is highly likely to result in financial losses unless there is a significant surplus from transfers. Additionally, a continuation of the low revenue growth reported in financial year (FY) 2018, coupled with a reduction in transfer profits, could leave clubs with high wage-to-revenue ratios heavily exposed and potentially lead to financial distress. This explains why the 70% ratio is included as a risk indicator in the UEFA Club Licensing and Financial Fair Play Regulations.
>
> (UEFA, 2020b)

As stated above, finding the right balance between revenues and costs and revenue optimisation and utilisation is very important for a football club to become a successful commercial organisation. Financial Management is seen as planning, organising, directing, and controlling the financial activities of a football club. To overcome the inherent uncertainty created by sporting results and the influence of external stakeholders (such as governing bodies, law enforcement, sponsors, change in ownership, and political scene) on the operations, football clubs need to prioritise the financial well-being and sustainability of the organisation. This can be done by mapping the revenue and cost structures within the club and by imposing a system of checks and balances in the financial operations.

Revenue: In general, the commercial revenue streams of clubs are mostly divided into three broad categories; transfers, media/broadcasting, and commercial. For example, in the Bundesliga, the revenue clubs receive from transfers and media is a big part of the overall income stream as stated in their financial report for the financial years (FY) 2017-2018. Of the €3.81bn total revenues, 32.72% comes from broadcasting, 22.86% from sponsorship, 14.12% from matchday revenue, 16.93% from transfers, and only 4.81% from merchandising (Bundesliga, 2018).

The revenue streams to focus on are those that are recurrent and controllable. Regarding revenue generation, clubs focus too much on the sporting results and profits made from player transfers. Focusing on the elements within your control (e.g. pricing, commercial offering, and quality) and mitigating against the elements which are not directly impressionable is the way forward. I consider revenues out of transfers a bonus on the club's yearly budget. When making up a budget, it is hardly impossible to be certain of the x-amount of income coming out of transfers. The number of players sold will differ in each transfer period. Relying on this type of income to be break-even is not sustainable over time. This situation is similar for income out of broadcasting, except these are recurrent for a certain cycle. However, football clubs do not have full control and need to adapt to the distribution model set by the league. So, again, when making up a budget, only consider the amount certain of. Any extras due to sporting achievement should be seen as an extra. This contains transfer revenues and UEFA club competition qualifying revenues and bonuses. Focus on the revenue streams you have an impact on and can therefore optimise. However, what are the costs to consider in preparing a football club's budget? I will disclose this under the commercial tag operations.

The principle of check and balances applies to football in the way that mismanagement, or even fraud, cannot occur. This requires a designated person to authorise purchases, payroll, and disbursements. Furthermore, separate handling of receipt and deposit functions from record-keeping functions should be in place. Purchasing functions should be separate from accounts payable functions. Additionally, the same person who writes a cheque should be different from the person who signs a cheque. Your club requires an independent check of work being done by a board member or an outside source if it is too small that duties cannot be separated. The club must have appointed a qualified finance officer who is responsible for its financial matters; UEFA describes that the finance officer must hold, as a minimum, one of the following qualifications:

- Diploma of a certified public accountant
- Diploma of qualified auditor
- Finance officer diploma issued by the licensor, or an organisation recognised by the licensor

## Football ownership and financial governance

In football, the emphasis on profit-making, often at the core of mainstream organisations, is routinely substituted with maximising on-field success. As such, football clubs have been 'leveraged by significant levels of debt often in the form of soft, interest-free loans from their owners with a high proportion of club revenue normally spent on player acquisitions and wages' (Plumley, 2019). A profit-making, and revenue-optimisation culture is not in place in every football organisation. One of the reasons behind this is the chosen management style and the expectations and ambitions of the owner.

PART I disclosed five types of ownership models in the football industry (profit-maximising owner, win-maximising owner, benefactor owner, socially responsible owner, and marketing owner). Profit-maximising owners are revenue generation focused.

An example of this is that, in some cases, football clubs have been acquired using leveraged buyouts (LBO). Most prominently is the acquisition of Manchester United in 2005 by the Glazer family. In the case of United, the Glazer family borrowed funds to acquire its majority stake in the club, securing part of the loan against the club's assets, with the club itself taking on the debt. The fact that not all the debt was secured resulted in higher interest rates thereon. The result of an LBO is that a substantial cost of the acquisition is effectively being met by those who provide cash flow to the club, its supporters, commercial partners, and media organisations. The dissatisfaction of many Manchester United fans was compounded further by the club's subsequent flotation on the New York Stock Exchange. This saw the club raise 250 million EURO through the issue of 16,7 million class A shares. These carry only one-tenth of the voting rights of existing shares in the company and no dividend rights. Only half of the proceeds of the issue was used to pay down the club's debts, the other half being returned directly to the Glazer family.

(Morrow, Football Economics and Finance, 2017a)

That United really has an ownership model based on revenue generation was confirmed in 2015 with the statement that

in fiscal 2016 we begin paying a regular quarterly cash dividend on our Class A and Class B ordinary shares of $0.045 per share. Recently the club's board of directors approved replacing the previous quarterly cash dividend with a regular semi-annual cash dividend of $0.09 per share. They expect to continue paying regular semi-annual dividends to their Class A ordinary shareholders and Class B ordinary shareholders out of their operating cash flows. The declaration and payment of any future dividends, however, will be at the sole discretion of the board of directors or a committee thereof, and the expectations and policies regarding dividends are subject to change as their business needs, capital requirements, or market conditions change.

(Manchester United FC, 2015)

For the year 2020, the total dividend distributed to the class A and B shareholders tallies up to more than 15 million euros. Although fans often rally against this type of ownership, wanting to extract money out of the club, these clubs usually avoid financial distress due to a strict system of financial processing and analysis.

The ownership structures with potentially the most alarming business model are the benefactors and marketing owners. Whenever they hold shares of the club and their personal and business goals are reached yearly, it will look like the club is progressing correctly. However, this concentrated ownership model (relying on one sole person or company) depends entirely on the owner's ability and willingness to continue to fund the club and cover the losses. An example of this is the Austrian football club WSG Swarovski Tirol. The club located in Innsbruck was promoted in 2019 to the Austrian Bundesliga. After promotion, the club announced that its name would be changed to WSG Swarovski Tirol, a decision taken by the board and the club's president Diana Langes-Swarovski (great-great-granddaughter of Daniel Swarovski, founder of Swarovski, the world-famous crystal manufacturer). Her investment originated through her high involvement in the direct community of the company's headquarters she partly inherited. Investing in the football club provides entertainment to the city and region. Furthermore, the spotlights are shining on the brand Swarovski owing to its presence in football. Is owning a club a real marketing asset for a company like Swarovski? The fact that the company's name is already mentioned seven times in this book proves that it resounds to people. What if the club would have still carried the name WSG Wattens? Probably nobody outside Austria would have heard of them. The risk for the club? When Diana leaves, the club cannot continue to run the operations as they currently are unless a similar investor replaces her.

## Financial fair play (FFP)

Although not the main focus of this book, the sporting side of managing a football club requires the most investments. It requires assembling a playing squad, composing a training staff, wages, equipment, and infrastructure. None of it is cheap. Take, for example, players' wages. In a normal company environment, a healthy wage-to-revenue ratio is between 10% and 30%, depending on the industry. Owing to the specific nature of the football industry (similar to other businesses in the entertainment industry), where athletes earn a decent amount for their efforts, a wage-to-revenue ratio lower than 60% seems reasonable. In reality, many football clubs exceed that percentage and even exceed a wage-to-revenue ratio of 70%, which UEFA describes as a situation highly likely to result in losses for the club. When looking at leagues with high sporting competitiveness and a high-pressure level to reach sporting results, the English Championship stands out. As Championship clubs are increasingly gambling to reach the top to promote to the Premier League eventually, wages are increasing severely. In the 2017/2018 season, player salaries in the Premier League saw significant growth, leading to record levels of wages. The overall increase was 8%, from £693 million to £748 million, equivalent to an extra £1.1 million a week. This growth was driven by the lure of the Premier League's riches and resulted in financially reckless behaviour by club owners.

It is important to note that the wage-to-revenue ratio measures a club's financial sustainability and efficiency. A ratio above 100% means the club is spending more on wages than it earns in revenues, putting itself at financial risk in the long term. Ideally, the wage-to-revenue ratio should be between 50% and 60%, with a ratio higher than 90% considered unsustainable and a ratio lower than 40% considered a poor use of resources.

In the 2018 Championship, the average wage-to-revenue ratio was 107%, highlighting the financial risk clubs are prepared to take to chase promotion to the Premier League. This type of financial management can lead to FFP issues and put a strain on the club's owners.

Clubs at high financial risk were Reading (197%), Derby (161%), Brentford (135%), Nottingham Forest (122%), and Preston (113%). In contrast, clubs with a more sustainable wage-to-revenue ratio included Sunderland (74%), Barnsley (76%), Leeds (77%), Burton (78%), and Middlesbrough (79%). These clubs either recently relegated or promoted to the Championship and typically have lower wage-to-revenue ratios (Football Club's annual accounts, 2018–2019).

The same conclusion can be made in the Belgian Pro League, where, owing to the play-offs, the number of places at the top is limited. Only four play-off places are available in the 2022–2023 season, and six to seven teams started the season with the ambition of playing those play-offs. The competitive balance, the combination of financial mismanagement, and trying to close the sporting gap with the Netherlands and Portugal have led to a situation in which the wage-to-revenue ratio could be healthier (Table 11.1).

It may not be surprising that in the FY 2021, the cumulative loss of all Belgian Pro League clubs exceeded €139M, and in FY 2022, that cumulative loss will be even higher.

Job Gulikers investigated the situation of PSV from the Eredivisie and found a similar issue. Owing to their financial situation, the club was forced to sell their top players, Cody Gakpo, to Liverpool FC and Noni Madueke to Chelsea FC in January 2023 while the club was still in the race to win the league. The reason for this was that the club prepared their budget with

Table 11.1 Wage-to-Revenue Ratio Pro League top 7 FY 2022
(Data from accounts Pro League Football Clubs, 2022)

| Football club | Wage-to-revenue ratio – FY 2022 (%) |
|---|---|
| • Club Brugge KV | 81 |
| • RSC Anderlecht | 150 |
| • KRC Genk | 80 |
| • Standard de Liège | 143 |
| • Antwerp FC | 102 |
| • KAA Gent | 107 |
| • Union Saint-Gilloise | 176 |

the thought of playing the Champions League every year, even though they did not qualify for the Champions League since 2018–2019. This resulted in an operational loss of €12M per year and an amortisation of €28M. A combined loss of €40M. It is believed that the COVID pandemic impacted the prudence club directors would handle their finances but on the contrary. Since the last pre-COVID season, the player wages have risen to 24% while the club's capital decreased from €40M to €17M (Graat, 2023).

In conclusion, the continued growth of player salaries led to a rise in overall wages and financially risky behaviour by club directors and owners. The wage-to-revenue ratio is a crucial measure of a club's financial sustainability and stability, and clubs should strive for a 60% or lower ratio. The high wage-to-revenue ratios of clubs like RSC Anderlecht, Reading, and Derby put them at risk of FFP issues and financial strain.

Financial Fair Play, as a means of promoting fiscal responsibility among clubs that participate in European club competitions, UEFA has established a set of FFP rules. These rules are enforced by UEFA for European club competitions and by individual football authorities, such as national associations and leagues, for domestic competitions. The FFP rules can be divided into two main categories. The first category places a limit on the maximum losses a football club can incur and is profit-related. The second category is linked to wage control and is typically set as either an absolute number or as a percentage of income (Maguire, Understanding Football Club Finance, 2020).

The primary objective of UEFA's FFP regulations is to encourage clubs to manage their financial operations more effectively and attain a sustainable balance between income, spending, and investment. These regulations became effective beginning in the 2013/2014 season and are based on clubs' financial results from the 2011/2012 season (Morrow, Football Economics and Finance, 2017b). To comply with the FFP regulations, clubs must ensure that their football-related expenses, including transfers and wages, are balanced by revenues generated by television and ticket sales, as well as commercial department income. Expenditures related to stadium improvements, training facilities, youth development, and community projects are exempt from this calculation (BBC Sport, 2019).

The most crucial requirement under the FFP regulations is that clubs must report a break-even position over a rolling three-year period. This break-even position is not an absolute position, but rather one that is subject to an acceptable level of deviation. Notably, these regulations do not assess the merits of particular ownership structures. The central requirement of a break-even position based on a comparison of relevant income and expenses restricts the ability of club owners to make contributions to cover losses or engage in ex-ante contributions other than in connection with specified investment activities. While the break-even requirement has received the most attention, UEFA has also reinforced other requirements in Club Licensing, especially those concerning clubs that have overdue payables to their employees, tax authorities, or other clubs (UEFA, 2012).

At least, these have been the regulations until UEFA announced the new financial sustainability regulations in April 2022. These new regulations have three pillars and have been applicable since June 2022.

1. No overdue payables rule
2. Football earnings rule
3. Squad cost rule

UEFA has recently introduced new regulations for clubs participating in UEFA competitions, which are based on three pillars: the No Overdue Payables Rule, the Football Earnings Rule, and the Squad Cost Rule.

The no overdue payables rule requires clubs to ensure that all payments due to employees, social and tax authorities, and other clubs have been paid in full by the relevant deadlines. This rule aims to promote fair financial practices and ensure that clubs meet their financial obligations in a timely manner.

The Football Earnings Rule requires clubs to generate their own revenues from football-related activities, such as matchday income, broadcasting rights, and sponsorship deals. This rule encourages clubs to become more self-sufficient and reduce their reliance on external sources of funding, such as wealthy owners or investors.

The Squad Cost Rule aims to limit the amount of money clubs can spend on player salaries, transfer fees, and player agents to 70% of club revenues by the 2025–2026 season. This rule requires clubs to balance their spending on player-related costs with their football-related earnings. Clubs that exceed the permitted level of spending will be subject to penalties, including fines, transfer bans, and potential exclusion from UEFA competitions (UEFA, 2022).

# Broadcasting revenue

For many clubs in European football, revenues from the collective (most of the leagues) or individual (some exceptions) sales of broadcasting rights make up a large portion of their total revenues. People like watching football on television, it is as simple as that. Over the years, rights holders, leagues, and broadcasters worked together to make the football product appealing. The more appealing the product, the more viewers and the more revenue that comes in. UEFA's Club Benchmarking Report shows that broadcasting has driven the most revenue growth for European football clubs from 2009 until 2018. Broadcasting has directly generated €4.2bn of revenue growth and has contributed the bulk of the additional €1.5bn revenue growth from UEFA competitions (UEFA, 2019).

As Kieran Maguire describes in his book, *The Price of Football: Understanding Football Club Finance* (2020), broadcasters see the football product as an extremely valuable product because of:

- The long period in time domestic competition runs, there is content from August until May.
- The sport is popular among a demographic that does not necessarily watch much television (males aged 15–34).
- The culture of advertising and sponsoring has been incorporated into the game for already a long period (people do not mind being bombarded with company logos).
- The exclusivity of the product (you need to have obtained the rights in order to even broadcast snapshots out of the game).
- The opportunity to re-sell parts of the rights to secondary media outlets.

- The possibility to organise events focused on the product to generate an extra revenue stream'.

(Maguire, *The Price of Football: Understanding Football Club Finance*, 2020)

Furthermore, this revenue stream is undergoing endless growth. For example the Belgian Pro League negations regarding the broadcasting of the matches of the First Division A (first tier) and First Division B (second tier); The Pro League negotiated the distribution of broadcasting rights with major national and international broadcasting companies while distributing the consequent revenues to the clubs via a predetermined split. In 2012, the total TV money was around 57 million euros. In 2015, this was 10 million euros more. Over the last (17/18) season, the contract was split between the traditional pay TV channels Proximus, Telenet, and VOO; this grew further to 80.9 million euros. As of the season 2020–2021, owing to the new broadcasting deal, the Pro League has struck with Eleven Sports (now part of DAZN), 103 million euros can be distributed yearly to the clubs. This means that from 2012 until 2020, there has been an uplift of 82%. It sounds like much money for Eleven Sports to still make a profit by only selling subscription services to an audience of 11 million, right?

How does this money eventually end up in the clubs' bank accounts? As leagues nowadays mostly sell broadcast rights collectively, they work with a distribution model to determine which piece of the pie belongs to which club. The distribution of broadcast income varies from country to country. Let us compare two countries: Spain and Germany. In Spain, clubs sold their broadcast rights individually to different media for a very long time. This gave the top clubs (most predominantly Real Madrid and FC Barcelona) a financial advantage over their competitors in the league. It created an absolute imbalance in the league's financial structure, with these top clubs earning approximately 140 million euros each from domestic broadcasting and smaller clubs (like, for example, Almeria, Granada, Malaga, and others) who were not able to make 20 million euros out of their deals. In 2015, and effective from season 16/17 onwards, the practice of individual selling was deemed illegal by the Spanish government. La Liga was then mandated to sell the rights for all clubs in the division. However, Real Madrid and Barcelona were protected to a certain degree, as the new regulations stated that no club could be worse off than before the changes were introduced (Maguire, Understanding Football Club Finance, 2020). Right now, the distribution

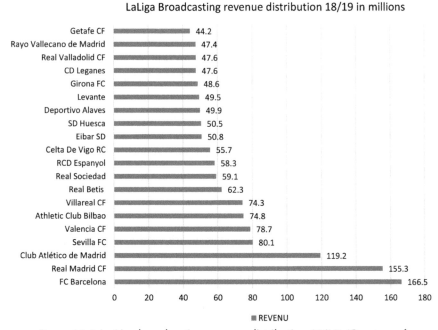

*Figure 11.1* La Liga broadcasting revenue distribution 18/19. (Courtesy of McMahon, 2019.)

model in Spain is as follows: 10% of TV rights revenue is given to second-tier Segunda B, with the remaining 90% divided so that 50% is equally shared between the league's 20 teams, 25% allocated according to results across the previous five seasons, and the final 25% distributed based on metrics such as the number of television subscribers and viewers per match. For the 2018/2019 season, this resulted in the following distribution (Figure 11.1).

In Germany, the DFL (Deutsche Fussball Liga) is responsible for the distribution of revenue out of broadcasting to all their member clubs playing in either the Bundesliga or 2. Bundesliga. For the 2018–2019 season, the total revenue from marketing media rights for matches in national and international competitions was about 1,740 million euros. For the seasons from 2017/2018 to 2020/2021 onwards, the Board of DFL Deutsche Fußball Liga has unanimously agreed on a new model for the distribution of media income.

The distribution of national broadcasting income, including proceeds from group marketing such as the official match ball and licensed products, will be guided by a new four-pillar model in the future. The new model considers elements of the current model, such as a five-year ranking of sports performance, but also applies additional parameters to all leagues.

Four pillars of the new model:

1. **Sustainability in Sports:** This pillar assesses a club's long-term contribution to the development of Bundesliga and Bundesliga 2 using a 20-year view.
2. **Young Talent:** This pillar rewards the deployment of U23 players for the first time.
3. **Competition:** This pillar aims to enhance the appeal of the various table regions.
4. **International Performance:** This pillar distributes 50% of the international income based on a five-year ranking of international performance.

Distribution of international income:

- 25% of the international income is distributed evenly among all 18 Bundesliga clubs.
- 50% of the international income is paid out based on a five-year ranking of international performance in proportion to the points awarded.
- 25% of the international income is based on the number of matches played in the Europe League and Champions League (including qualifying competitions), proportional to the number of points achieved.

In comparison with UEFA's Five-Year Ranking System: The new model has differences in its calculation methods compared to UEFA's system, including the absence of bonus points for reaching the group phase in international competitions.

*Bundesliga 2*

Beginning with the 2017/2018 season, Bundesliga 2 will receive an annual share of five million euros of the international income before the Bundesliga clubs receive any. This amount will increase by one million euros each season. The DFL Board chose a differentiated solution instead of the previous categories, which resulted in a rigid distribution of the proceeds between the leagues. The board also decided not to implement criteria such as the number of fans and viewer ratings, as these factors were found to be difficult to measure and compare after extensive investigation. The new four-pillar model for distributing the national broadcasting income has been introduced to incorporate elements of the current model and include additional parameters across all leagues.

1. Pillar 1 'Standard': This pillar accounts for 70% of the national income and is distributed using the existing formula. The formula evaluates the past five seasons of the Bundesliga and Bundesliga 2 clubs, with a ratio of 5:4:3:2:1 starting from the most recent season. The highest-ranked Bundesliga club will receive 5.8% of the income, and the lowest-ranked is 2.9%. In Bundesliga 2, the first club will receive 1.69% and the last 0.75%.

2. Pillar 2 'Sustainability in Sports': This pillar accounts for 5% of the national income and is distributed based on a 20-year ranking of the sporting performance of all 36 clubs, including both Bundesliga and Bundesliga 2. All seasons, are given equal weighting, starting with the most recent one.

3. Pillar 3 'Young Talent': This pillar accounts for 2% of the national income and is distributed proportionally to the number of minutes U23 players trained by German clubs are on the field in the current season. All matches, excluding relegations and extra time, are considered, including those in the season in which the player turns 23. Foreign players must register with a club within the DFB territory before turning 18.

4. Pillar 4 'Competition': This pillar distributes 23% of the national income and is based on a weighted five-year ranking (5:4:3:2:1) of the individual table regions, including all 36 clubs. The ranking differs from Pillar 1 in the calculation methods applied, and the first six clubs receive the same amount.

(Bundesliga, 2017)

This new approach to the distribution resulted in the following amounts paid out to the clubs participating in the German Bundesliga at the end of the 21/22 season (Figure 11.2).

Will these numbers keep growing, and what is the future of broadcasting rights? Keiran Maguire discussed in *The Price of Football: Understanding Football Club Finance* that

> Football is one of the few crown jewels still held by traditional television broadcasters as they are certainly not going to give up their prize assets without a fight. Take, for example, Sky YV is owned by American giant ComCast. They have a business model dependent upon fans renewing their subscriptions annually.

(Maguire, *The Price of Football: Understanding Football<br>Finance*, 2020)

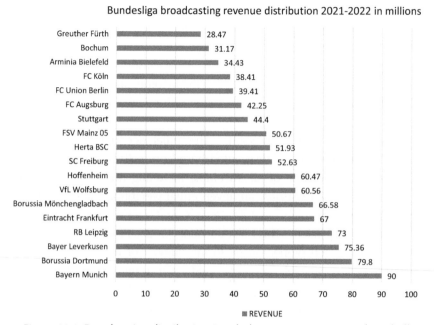

Bundesliga broadcasting revenue distribution 2021-2022 in millions

| Club | Revenue |
|------|---------|
| Greuther Fürth | 28.47 |
| Bochum | 31.17 |
| Arminia Bielefeld | 34.43 |
| FC Köln | 38.41 |
| FC Union Berlin | 39.41 |
| FC Augsburg | 42.25 |
| Stuttgart | 44.4 |
| FSV Mainz 05 | 50.67 |
| Herta BSC | 51.93 |
| SC Freiburg | 52.63 |
| Hoffenheim | 60.47 |
| VfL Wolfsburg | 60.56 |
| Borussia Mönchengladbach | 66.58 |
| Eintracht Frankfurt | 67 |
| RB Leipzig | 73 |
| Bayer Leverkusen | 75.36 |
| Borussia Dortmund | 79.8 |
| Bayern Munich | 90 |

*Figure 11.2* Broadcasting distribution Bundesliga 21/22. (Courtesy of Football Finance, 2022.)

This is a very traditional approach; no guarantee that this will stay the same over time. Consumer behaviour changes, and so the product needs to change. DAZN and Eleven Sports were two newcomers to the market. They came in with a bang, afterward slowed down, but still are active in the US, German, Italian, and Belgian market, as in different Asian markets. In 2022, DAZN acquired Eleven Sports. Lately, we have seen the introduction of Apple in the market with the acquisition of the MLS (Major League Soccer) broadcasting rights. Does this mean the other GAMMA companies will also enter the scene? Two tendencies can be derived from these new initiatives: (1) OTT (over-the-top) services and (2) technological innovations, "such as the Borussia Dortmund example with the virtual boarding" (ironSource, 2022).

An 'over-the-top' media service is any online content provider that offers streaming media as a standalone product. The term is commonly applied to video-on-demand platforms but also refers to audio streaming, messaging services, or internet-based voice calling solutions. OTT services circumvent traditional media distribution channels such as telecommunications networks or cable television providers. The complete service can be accessed at your leisure as long as there is access to an internet connection — either locally or through a mobile network. OTT services are typically monetized via paid subscriptions, but there are exceptions. For example, some OTT platforms might offer in-app purchases or advertising.

(ironSource, 2022)

The emergence of 'over-the-top' (OTT) service providers, such as Amazon Prime in the UK or DAZN in Germany and Italy, into football rights bidding, will likely shift the football rights broadcasting landscape (KPMG, 2020). OTT content is compatible with multiple devices, allowing users to watch from various gadgets. This enables fans to watch from any imaginable location, given that they have Internet access. Moreover, additional content, such as betting on games, can be integrated into the stream. Another major advantage of the technology is that although the user has many alternatives, streaming services are offered for considerably lower prices compared to traditional products such as cable TV packages, where the content is provided according to a fixed schedule, and the consumer has to adapt. Next to a lower price for the end consumer, content can be delivered in multiple ways and individualised for single-consumer purposes.

Although for all the football leagues in Europe, their domestic market stays the most important in revenue generation. The EPL (English Premier League) is mostly watched in England over any other single country, La Liga in Spain, Bundesliga in Germany, and Serie A in Italy. Nevertheless, domestic market revenue will eventually come to a limit. Therefore, football clubs are looking into exploring different international markets through technological innovations. Borussia Dortmund, for example, has invested in a Virtual Advertising Display System. Since the start of the 2018/2019 season, BVB (Borussia Dortmund) has been the first and only Bundesliga club to use cutting-edge technology that allows for the multiplication of advertising displayed at home games, all without the creation of a single square centimetre of additional advertising space in Signal Iduna Park. The club's virtual display system allows the advertising displayed on TV broadcasts in the United States to be different from that in Europe – or indeed different from that in Asia too. Meanwhile, fans back in Germany are entirely oblivious. This is a huge step for clubs and leagues to generate sponsorship income via broadcasting and tackle new markets with relevant content.

# Commercial operations: income & costs

As stated above, football clubs should focus on the elements within revenue generation that they can control. Income streams out of transfers are not recurrent and are not the same every year; therefore, we see these forms of revenue as extra. Adding up to a club's budget. I believe the following balance can be seen as ideal and healthy by considering the financial operation and economic reality of small, midsized, and large clubs (Figure 11.3).

Hereunder is a list of potential revenue streams under the categories mentioned above. While thinking about the different revenue streams, think back to the continuous circle, which we explained earlier in part one. It enhances creative thoughts on how a football club can optimise its brand identity and, eventually, its revenue streams (Table 11.2).

While analysing the different costs at a football club, categorising those costs became a real challenge. Often, operational costs are categorised in the sporting category to keep a better overview of sporting and business budgets. One 'cost' we would like to point out is 'savings'. As football clubs often only realise the net result at the end of the financial year, it would be smart to allocate a certain percentage of the total revenue to the club's savings or net reserve. We have learned from the COVID crisis that anything can happen, which can greatly impact clubs' revenues. Therefore clubs should be prepared for a disaster at any moment and ideally have enough savings to carry the fixed costs for a full year (Table 11.3).

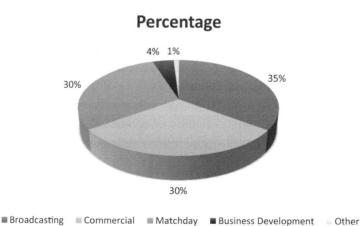

*Figure 11.3* Balanced revenue streams for football clubs

Table 11.2 Different revenue streams for a football club

| Broadcasting | Commercial revenue | Matchday revenue | Business development | Other |
|---|---|---|---|---|
| • National Competition | • Merchandising | • Season tickets | • Business investments | • Solidarity Payments |
| • National Cup competition | • Licensing | • Solo tickets | • Acquisitions | • Training compensation |
| • UEFA Club Competitions | • Sponsorships | • Hospitality | • Mergers | • Subsidies |
| • Streaming | • Naming rights | • Food & Beverages | | • Transfers |
| | • Visibility | • Sky boxes | | |
| | • Partnerships | • Stadium Events | | |
| | • Activations | | | |
| | • Non-stadium events | | | |
| | • Memberships | | | |

Table 11.3 Different costs for a football club categorised

| Sporting | | Business | | | |
|---|---|---|---|---|---|
| Wages | Operational | Business | Operational Costs | Wages | Other |
| • Players | • Pitch maintenance | • Office material | • Matchday | • Employees | • Social Secretary |
| • Coaching Staff | • Youth academy | • Marketing & promotion | • Car leasing | • Lawyer fees | • Road taxes |
| • Player Agents | • Equipment | • Brochures | • Agencies | • Accountancy | • Environmental taxes |
| • Insurance | • Training kit | • LED boarding | • Transport | • Freelancers | • National social security offices |

(Continued)

*Table 11.3 Continued*

| Sporting | | Business | | | |
|---|---|---|---|---|---|
| Wages | Operational | Business | Operational Costs | Wages | Other |
| • Social contribution | • Gym | • Relationship gifts | • Venue Maintenance | • Volunteers | • Withholding taxes |
| • Social Secretary | • Nutrition | • Merchandise Stock | • Water & electricity | • Insurance | • Restaurants |
| • Civil liability | • Hotel & travel costs | | • Mobile & Internet | • Social contribution | • Subscriptions |
| | • Education | | • Hospitality | • Social secretary | • Savings |
| | • Training Centre | | • Website & IT | • Civil liability | |
| | | | • Software | | • **Investments** |
| | | | • Installations & machinery | | • Apartments |
| | | | • Security | | • Nonfootball-related businesses |
| | | | • Hardware | | |
| | | | • Stadium rent | | |

## Structuring a club's economy: red flags

Often the biggest mistakes in controlling a football club from a financial point of view are made on the sporting side. Football club owners do not take the time to build their team to the ranking position they admire. They want immediate success, which is something that is costly. For example, in the English Championship, the promoting clubs spends over 120% of revenues on player wages, aiming to hit the Premier League jackpot in broadcasting revenues. Even football clubs spending more than 70% of revenue on salaries, wages, signing bonuses, employee benefits, and social taxes take a big risk as their main/only focus is on the sporting side. This way of management does not build a long sustainable model for the club. Another example is after a club acquisition; the new owner goes crazy on the transfer market, as we have seen with Todd Boehly, who acquired Chelsea FC in the summer of 2022. The club spent €611,49 million on new players in his first two transfer windows. An absolute record in the history of football.

A second red flag is the amount of money being spent on player agents. A well-structured scouting system is often cheaper and better in the long run than working only with player agents. A player agent is not a scout but represents a player or football club. Being dependent on which football players a player agent brings forward is a dangerous business as it will be the only option left. In the Belgian Pro League, they spend over € 34 million on player agent fees during season 2020–2021 (Deloitte, 2022).

A thirds red flag for a football club's financial situation depends on broadcasting revenues. Suppose broadcasting revenues cover over 60–90% of the total revenue. In that case, it means that when a football club is being relegated and the broadcasting revenues decrease by half or even more, the club will face financial difficulties and has a high risk of going bankrupt. What are possible solutions?

Stick to the budget, even if things do not go as planned on the sporting side. Do not make emotional decisions if the club is fighting against relegation. Work on a long-term plan to increase the budget by increasing matchday and commercial revenues. Become unreliable from player agents by investing in a youth academy and a strong scouting department working with data. To conclude, focus on strategic planning and trust the process.

## Key takeaways

- Wage-to-revenue ratio should be 60% or lower.
- Do not be too reliant on one revenue stream but have multiple equal revenue sources.
- Control costs! Never spend money that you do not have.
- The highest costs are transfer fees, player agent fees, and wages. Having a smart strategy for these costs helps to stay within budget.

- Savings will help the club through difficult and unforeseen times, such as a pandemic or economic crisis.
- Invest apart from non-recurrent revenue streams, such as transfers, in new businesses that generate an extra income for the club.

# References

BBC Sport. (2019, March 8). *Sport Football*. Retrieved from BBC: https://www.bbc.com/sport/football/29361839

Bundesliga. (2017). *Media Distribution*. Retrieved from Bundeslige: https://www.bundesliga.com/en/news/Bundesliga/agmd12-dfl-media-income-distribution-424720.jsp

Bundesliga. (2018). *FInancial Report*. Bundesliga.

Deloitte. (2019). *Annual Review of Football Finance*. Deloitte.

Deloitte. (2022). *Socio-economische impact studie van de Pro League op de Belgische economie*. Deloitte.

Football Club's Annual Accounts. (2018–2019). *Annual Accounts*.

Football Finance. (2022). Retrieved from Football Finance: https://football-finance.com/1-bundesliga-tv-revenue-distribution/

Graat, J. (2023, Januari 30). *Financieel riskant beleid*. Retrieved from Trouw: https://www.trouw.nl/sport/financieel-riskant-beleid-gerbrands-ten-grondslag-aan-crisis-psv~bd46d441/

ironSource. (2022, Augustus 23). Retrieved from is.com: https://www.is.com/glossary/ott/

KPMG. (2020). *Will OTT Shake up the Football Broadcasting Industry*. KPMG Football Benchmark.

Maguire, K. (2020). Understanding Football Club Finance. In K. Maguire, *The Price of Football: Understanding Football Club Finance* (p. 224). Agenda Publishing.

Manchester United FC. (2015). Retrieved from Investor Relations Manchester United: ir.manutd.com

McMahon, B. (2019, December 15). Retrieved from Forbes: https://www.forbes.com/sites/bobbymcmahon/2019/12/15/la-liga-distributes-14b-in-tv-money-barcelona-and-17-other-teams-receive-record-payouts/

Morrow, S. (2017a). Football Economics and Finance. In K. M. J. Hughson, *Routledge Handbook of Football Studies* (p. 164). London: Taylor & Francis.

Morrow, S. (2017b). Football Economics and Finance. In K. M. J.Hughson, *Routledge Handbook of Football Studies* (p. 167). London: Taylor & Francis.

Plumley, R. W. (2019). Finance and Accounting in Football. In D. P. S. Chadwick, *Routledge Handbook of Football Business and Management* (p. 186). London: Francis & Taylor.

Pro League Football Clubs. (2022). *Financial Accounts*.

UEFA. (2012). *Financial Fair Play and Club Licensing Regulations*. Nyon.

UEFA. (2019). *Club Benchmarking Report*. UEFA.

UEFA. (2020a). *Club Licensing Benchmark Report*. UEFA.

UEFA. (2020b). *Club Licensing Benchmarking Report*. UEFA.

UEFA. (2022, April 7). *Financial Sustainability Regulations*. Retrieved from UEFA.com: https://www.uefa.com/insideuefa/news/0274-14da0ce4535d-fa5b130ae9b6-1000--explainer-uefa-s-new-financial-sustainability-regulations/

# 12 Strategic planning

At the beginning of part III, we highlighted that no matter the ownership model or the owner's aspirations, board of directors, or investors, a balance should be found between the three focus areas (commercial, sporting, and social) of football club management. To achieve this balance, the five building blocks should come together in a strategic plan. A phased, long-term overview of where the management aims to bring the club over the next years.

The main difference between a football club and a regular for-profit organisation is that in a football club, decisions are often made based on emotions, short-term results, and public pressure. When you are winning on the pitch, internal and external stakeholders automatically assume that everything is well organised and managed. Yet, this is not always the case. The perfect example of this could be found in Belgium at the end of the 2015/2016 season. Royal White Star Brussels was crowned champion of the 2nd division by having one point more than the number two, KAS Eupen. Everything going well, right? Not really. At the end of the season, Royal White Star Brussels was not granted a licence to play in the first division. Rightfully, the Royal Belgian Football Associations (RBFA) and the Belgian Arbitration Court for Sports did not give the club a licence to play. Why? At the end of the season, the club could not pay back its short- and long-term financial obligation – Belgian media outlets reported an overall loss of more than 10 million EURO. They had no stadium to play in due to the commune of Molenbeek (Brussels) complaint regarding a systemic lack of maintenance and their general manager facing criminal charges.

DOI: 10.4324/9781003312680-15

Is winning on the pitch equal to winning off the pitch? Clearly not. It is necessary to have a long-term strategy where you forecast different scenarios, set multiple KPIs (Key Performance Indicators), and implement management tools to become a sustainable football club.

In your strategic plan, you should focus mainly on three questions; 'what do we do internally to create a new external direction?', 'How will we make use of means and people? How do we fit in the five main building blocks?'.

The term strategy may have multiple definitions, although it generally concerns the creation of plans to attain certain objectives over a longer period with the allotment of the necessary resources. The strategic plan outlines the organisation's vision and covers a period of 4–5 years. As football clubs are almost always multi-business organisations, the choices made by leaders in the strategic management process are characterised by much uncertainty. Strategic management often relies on formal analytical tools and processes. It is one of the challenges of managing a football club and why you cannot compare it to running a normal business. Football club owners and directors often underestimate the sporting uncertainty, emotional involvement, and pressure from external stakeholders such as media and fans. For that reason, a detailed strategic plan is crucial for the club's stability.

Strategy goes beyond simply setting aims of being the best; it should be about establishing what makes a club unique and leveraging those competitive advantages. An ideology can be formed considering what the club's brand is all about, what the club's consumers are looking for, which regulations are in place, and the financial situation. Getting all stakeholders to share this ideology is your end goal. This always works top-bottom and inside-out. Top-bottom: president and top management bring this ideology over to everyone inside the organisation by creating a culture. Inside-out: everyone in the club is an ambassador to ensure all outside stakeholders are on board as well.

What does a strategic process look like? Five activities should be considered: strategic analysis, strategic goal(s) formulation, strategic development planning, strategic implementation methods, and strategic evaluation mechanisms (Figure 12.1).

*Figure 12.1* **Five steps of a strategic process (see Heylen, 2016)**

1. **Strategic analysis:** Strategic management of football organisations involves formulating specific and articulated goals and objectives, designing action plans on how best to reach those goals, and allocating resources to implement those plans effectively. The strategic management system will work best if these strategies and plans are based on a profound understanding of the organisation's external environment and objectively appraising its internal resources and capabilities. Always start with an analysis of the internal and external context.

   - **Internal context:**

   Where, as a football organisation, are we today?

   To define this, a clear overview of the resources and capabilities should be given. Recourses can be described as tangible (land, stadium, equipment, financial resources,...) and intangible assets (brands, reputation, knowledge and experience, customer loyalty...) of the organisation. Capabilities are processes, systems, or organisational routines to coordinate resources for productive use.

   - **External context:**

   The external context is defined by non-susceptible environmental factors. Who are your customers? Who are competitors on the horizon? What kind of region are you in? How is the economic situation? In the increasingly complex and competitive environment football clubs are operating, knowing what can be controlled is as important as knowing what cannot. Only try to control what is controllable and be aware of the rest.

   The output of this exercise can serve as a starting point or measure the actual results of the club/academy against its intended goals and objectives. Therefore, there is no right time to do this exercise. It can be done throughout several phases the club will go through: new ownership, new management, new business pillars, or an intermediate evaluation. For example: doing a strategic analysis in the acquisition process of the club by a new owner can save the owner lots of headaches. The question 'Where do we want to go?' highly depends on which of the five business model ownerships the club has in place: profit-maximalisation, win-maximalisation, benefactor, social, or marketing. Not every business model ownership fits at every football club, so potential owners should have a clear overview of internal and external factors. The football club culture is way too important to neglect and will always cause a heated situation when there is no fit with the ambition of the new owner.

2. **Strategic goal formulation:**

The process of composing goals and objectives is the next phase in developing a strategic plan. For the strategic plan to succeed, the goals and objectives should be SMART: specific, measurable, achievable, relevant, and time bound. These goals should be made department-independently and cross-departmentally. The complex nature of a football club has the effect that goals are rarely achieved by one department only; departments and people working together on several challenges are key. Which goals should be set? There is no model, framework, or recipe to set the right ones. Clubs can certainly learn a great deal by exchanging views and ideas, but ultimately, to succeed, your goals should be your goals. They will help bridge where you are as a club now and where you want to be.

3. **Strategic development planning:**

Once the vision, goals, and objectives have been formulated, specific steps and activities must be developed and documented. Due to the time-consuming nature of this step, it is often neglected by a football club's management. Nevertheless, just because development planning may seem tedious and detailed, it plays a crucial role in successfully implementing strategies. As often for any organisation, it is possible to reach its objectives through different ways and means; leveraging the experience and ideas of employees and managers can be of great help. If in this phase, strategic planning is seen as a one-person job, it will lead to tunnel vision which can result in certain goals and objectives not being met.

A great example of building different scenarios can be seen in promotion and relegation management. The Royal Dutch Football Association provides promotion and relegation candidates with an overview of what can be expected upon relegation or promotion (KNVB Expertise, 2019). The federations support these clubs in making the right decisions in their strategic plans now that the club faces a new environment. We know it is difficult to believe, but almost no football club has a plan ready for when they are relegated. The reason is that they always believe it will happen to the other club but not to them.

According to the KNVB (Royal Dutch Football Association), there are three different levels for a club to prepare for a potential relegation or promotion:

- **Structural:** Always have a potential relegation or promotion in mind
- **Strategic:** Have a plan ready when promotion or relegation becomes a possibility
- **Operational:** After promotion or relegation to implement the plan and foreseen changes

Promotion or relegation should be something to keep in mind at all times, even for top football clubs who have not been in the relegation zone for decades. It is always good to have a backup plan. This does not necessarily have to be on the operational side, but from a legal perspective; it is something to tackle in contracts. Think about labour agreements, sponsor contracts, and stadium leases. Difficult situations can be prevented through such clauses. It takes a long time during a season before a club is mathematically safe for relegation. This means that many clubs are uncertain for most of the season, and relegation is a potential danger for a long time. Yet, they do not have a plan ready for when it happens.

The KNVB also explains that football clubs that promote or relegate will go through a process of four different phases. These phases are:

- **Expectations:** Prepare different scenarios and plans of action. Often done during the winter break in January.
- **Processing:** Create a detailed plan of action and set deadlines. As soon as relegation or promotion is happening, for sure.
- **Preparation:** Execute the plan of action and prepare next season.
- **Execution:** Implement operational changes.

An important advice from the KNVB is also to prepare a shadow budget. Within this budget, multiple scenarios are being processed. This will also come in handy when documents must be prepared for the licensing committee. Upon promotion, one of the biggest challenges is finding qualitative employees to help the club prepare for next season in a higher division. Therefore, it is important to have a clear strategy in each department like human resources.

4. **Strategic implementation methods:**

Now that you have designed a clear action plan and understand the outcome of different scenarios which will lead to accomplishing the different goals of the organisation, it is time to act. While effective strategy implementation depends greatly on how well the strategies have been formulated, well-formulated strategies do not automatically translate into the desired results. A common thread is a failure by management to understand that the organisations do not function by themselves fully but through individuals (employees, volunteers, service providers, and contractors). Strategy implementation depends on how well these individuals are activated to produce the desired results for the organisation. Effective organisation activation and as a result strategy implementation depends on how effectively the plan is communicated and shared within the organisation and across stakeholders, whether appropriate organisational structures support the strategy, and whether the people who must move the implementation forward are made responsible, accountable, and incentivised (Draeybe, 2020). The process leading up to making the appropriate action can be designed by a simple method; Plan → Do → Check → Act / Adjust ← Repeat.

The PDCA cycle is a model to guide continuous improvement and renewal in an organisation. The four letters stand for Plan, Do, Check, and Act. The cyclical nature ensures that quality improvement is continuously under consideration. It is assumed that implementing the PDCA cycle can achieve a higher quality of products or services.

The PDCA cycle (PAK, n.d.) consists of four steps and is explained as stated below:

- **Plan**: In this step, a plan is drawn up in which the results are clearly described. The objectives must be formulated SMART following the interests of the various stakeholders. In addition, the preconditions and the available resources must be clear.
- **Do**: This step concerns the execution and realisation of the approved plan. During the implementation, the activities and performances are continuously recorded and assessed.
- **Check**: In this step, the results achieved are compared with those the organisation had in mind. The differences are evaluated, and the causes of possible differences are identified.
- **Act**: In this step, after discovering differences in results, management makes adjustments. Management takes measures to achieve the planned results.

The purpose of implementing the PDCA cycle is to ensure that employees are continuously working on improvements. By improving quality, expenditure will be reduced and productivity increased. In practice, applying the PDCA cycle is complex. Formulating plans and implementing the corresponding action points is done, but the cycle is not completed because results are often not evaluated and guaranteed. Results must be evaluated to be adjusted if necessary and then start again with the first step.

5. **Strategic evaluation mechanisms:**

Evaluation is key to success. If you have no clue how you are performing, you will have no idea whether you are working correctly. Keeping track of how you are performing should not be difficult as you have earlier defined your objectives clearly. Go back to the organisational structure and the objectives of the owner. If you have a business model of profit-maximisation ownership, your number one KPI is profit. If the business model is win-maximisation ownership, your number one KPI is on-pitch performance and athlete management. If you have a benefactor model in place, your number one KPI is focused on stakeholder satisfaction. If you are socially focused, your number one KPI is giving back to society, and if you are focused on marketing, your number one KPI should be designed to improving other's brand value.

These general objectives should be tailored to everyone in the organisation. Individual managers will need to be assigned and made responsible for specific tasks and targets. A common tool used by many organisations to outline these responsibilities is management by objectives (MBO). MBO is establishing a management information system to compare actual performance and achievements to the defined objectives. Practitioners claim that the major benefits of MBO are that it improves employee motivation and commitment and allows for better communication between management and employees (Hayes, 2022).

Mikkel Draebye, described how strategic management is evolving within the football industry:

strategic management is the bread and butter of success in football organisations. Ambitious but realistic goals, analysis-based decisions, and plans together with continuous measurement and improvement systems will put football clubs in a position to increase their chances for grinding themselves to success.

(Draeybe, 2020)

But what cannot be forgotten (and what has been proved over the last year due to the outbreak and aftermath of COVID-19) is that the world is changing.

From a technological, legal, and competitive perspective, football organisations are in disturbing times. The importance of modern data collection cannot be hidden, and even smaller football clubs are feeling the need to keep innovating and using new technologies to win the interest of the fans. Social media and other communication technologies have existed for not even a decade, and already, new things like web3 is coming fast right after we say the rise and downfall of tokens and NFTs. The importance of the strategy is to remember that not all that is innovation brings value to an organisation. Keep the long-term vision in mind and involve external experts to guide you through difficult decisions.

## Key takeaways

- Formulate specific and articulated goals and objectives.
- Set key performance indicators based on your ownership business model.
- Dare to be critical about your organisation and dare to take harsh decisions.
- Implement the PDCA cycle with a defined timeline.

## References

Draeybe, M. (2020). Strategic Management in Football Organisations. In S. Chadwick, *Routledge Handbook of Football Business and Management* (p. 644). Taylor & Francis.

Hayes, A. (2022, August 30). *Management by Objectives*. Retrieved from Investopedia: https://www.investopedia.com/terms/m/management-by-objectives.asp

Heylen, R. (2016). Strategic Management.

KNVB Expertise. (2019). *Handboek Promotie en Degradatie Betaald Voetbal*. KNVB.

PAK. (n.d.). *PDCA Cyclus*. Retrieved from pak-organisatieontwikkeling: https://pak-organisatieontwikkeling.nl/inspiratie/pdca-cyclus-plan-do-check-act/

# 13 | Marketing and media

Although often ignored by general managers and the finance department, the football marketer should be at the heart of the football club. Returning to the beginning of this part, we highlighted that a brand would be the personality of a club if a club were a person. When a brand manager is responsible for making sure that one's personality is not going schizophrenic by positioning it well and by nurturing it over time through all layers of the club, a marketer will be able to exploit that personality. Considering that football clubs are a love brand – meaning consumers already love the brand for the brand – it is easy to know why we call this chapter the coolest in this book.

Although it sounds sexy, a job as a marketer in the football industry is not easy. A football club is a love brand; people love the club unconditionally, but the pressure is always there. When the sporting results are good, stadiums will be full, more merchandising will be sold, food and beverage revenues will increase, and social media comments will all be positive. However, if the team does not perform, all of the above turns negative. It is, therefore, very difficult to judge a marketer quickly. However, to know if a football club is doing a great job in marketing? Ask three questions:

1.  Are the football club's consumers/fans still talking about the club in the way the club prefers them to speak, even when on-the-pitch results are bad?
2.  Does the club positively affect its consumers to buy on the different channels they operate?
3.  Are the club and its products still relevant for present and future consumers?

DOI: 10.4324/9781003312680-16

The American Marketing Association defines marketing as the activity, set of institutions, and processes for creating, communicating, delivering, and exchanging offerings that value customers, clients, partners, and society (American Marketing Association, 2017). Going back to the basic definition results in what sports marketers should remember; it is all about the consumer, creating value, and offering them the opportunity to enter the sales funnel.

Esteve Calzada (Show me the money!, 2013), Chief Commercial Officer at City Football Group and former Head of Marketing at FC Barcelona, sees money-making as the 'raison d'être' of sports marketing. For sure, he is right. Attraction towards the club should be the priority to create and strengthen a market around the football club. A marketer can stir up the overall interaction with the club as an entity by using brand values. Brand marketing influences the decisions of a variety of customers, including both end-consumers and businesses. It is most effective for developing repeat business, as customers' perception of a brand will be largely informed by their previous experience(s) with that brand. This is the start of the marketer towards making money for his or her football club. Setting up campaigns to target groups (B2C and B2B) to buy the club's offerings and measuring the impact of these campaigns completes the to-do list of the marketing department. Although the outcome and goals within these types of marketing are differentiated, the basic set-up is the same: an accurate implementation of the 7 Ps of marketing. In a football environment, the marketing mix can be seen as a tool the head of marketing uses to help determine product and brand offerings. A football club must have all these elements before going to market. To stress the importance of planning, we highlight an example of groundwork gone wrong at each step of the 7P process.

7P's in football marketing:

1. **Product:** The Product should be compliant with what the consumers are expecting to get. Therefore, it is crucial to analyse all offerings from a B2C and B2B point of view. Marketing and sales must have a well-defined product. For example: The Club SD Eibar has been working on its strategy to make the club and the city of Eibar known internationally. With the help of LaLiga's global strategy, Eibar appeared in articles, reports, and interviews in prestigious media such as *The New York Times*, *The Guardian*, *11 Freunde*, and *Aljazeera*. However, after several activations abroad, the financial and commercial returns stayed low. Why?

SD Eibar is a very local club tied to the border of the Basque Country, and their product offering is not extremely relevant for an international crowd. After deciding to work with local people in foreign markets, they adjusted the product with a breakthrough in selected markets such as India and Japan.

2. **Place:** The product should be available where the target consumers are most convenient to shop. For example, the most loyal fans would be easily convinced to buy the newly released jersey each year. However, there must be a sales point. Owing to the outbreak and aftermath of COVID-19, many countries closed non-essential shops; for example, fan shops were closed in several countries for a long time. The importance and relevance of e-commerce, therefore, boomed during COVID; in other words, if there was no web shop, there were no sales.

3. **Price:** The Product should always represent good value for money. This does not necessarily mean it should be the cheapest available; one of the main tenets of the marketing concept is that customers are usually happy to pay more for something that works well for them. However, do not misuse it. It is not because football is a love brand that consumers should be charged whatever amount. Furthermore, football enthusiasts are rather traditional when it comes to pricing. For example: In 2012, Derby County FC was the first Football League club to offer 'demand-based' ticket pricing after joining Digonex and Tickets.com. The club used Digonex's Sports and Entertainment Analytical Ticketing System (SEATS), a system for event ticketing that scientifically changes prices based on econometric and behavioural principles. Prices fluctuated daily according to the team's form, the opposition, the day of the week, and the weather. However, the Rams ultimately decided to scrap dynamic pricing due to disinterest from fans, opting instead for a fixed pricing model (Derby County FC, 2012).

4. **Promotion:** Advertising, public relations, sales promotion, personal selling, and in more recent times, social media are all key communication tools for an organisation. Nothing is worse than using these types of media so that the organisation's message to its audiences is done in a manner they do not feel is appropriate, whether informative or appealing to their emotions. For example, LinkedIn is a social media channel focussed on professional contacts, brand or company updates, and B2B sales. A football club should embrace the specific characteristics of this platform. The evolution of Burnley Football Club, in this case, is

quite impressive. Two years ago, they struggled to get five likes on their LinkedIn content. Recently, they shifted from content formats that only focussed on sporting achievements to sharing socio-economic stories on the club's welfare. This has grasped the attention of this channel's users.

5. **People:** All clubs rely on the people who manage the day-to-day operations, from front-line sales staff to the managing director. As discussed earlier in chapter 2, having the right people is essential. Respectfully treating staff, even during tough times, is key. For example, acute economic downfall owing to COVID-19 was unforeseen, not financially estimated, and not covered by insurance. For many clubs, cost-cutting was the way to minimise losses in the short run. Two expenditure items were directly being questioned: players' wages and personnel remuneration. Juventus FC, West Ham United, Celtic Glasgow, Borussia Monchengladbach, and Olympique Lyon all decided to plunge into the possibility of a wage cut for players and technical staff. Other clubs, including Premier League giants Tottenham Hotspur FC, Liverpool FC, Sheffield United FC, Newcastle United FC, and Bournemouth AFC, suggested placing commercial and operational staff members on furlough leave. These measures were nothing more than a quick fix, saving some money on the very moderate wages of non-technical staff. This may not be the ideal way of treating people who invested so many working hours to benefit the club and its welfare.

6. **Processes:** The delivery to a football club is usually done with the customer present. Therefore, how the service is delivered is once again part of what the consumer is paying for. Buying a ticket nowadays is more than just going to the stadium, watching the game, and having a beer. Younger fans want more; they want to be entertained. For example: In 2016, West Ham United (WHU) moved from the iconic Upton Park to the Olympic Stadium. For the fans to be welcomed in their new home, WHU charged CSM Live with the task of making the stadium feel more like home by adding huge concourse displays of their former captains, crests, and record breakers. After consulting fans, the club realised that supporters felt that the stadium in Stratford lacked a West Ham touch and wanted to see more of the club's heritage displayed around the stadium. The topics of the three displays, unveiled before the game against Manchester United, were chosen via a fan vote. They show a timeline of how the club crest has changed, club legends that have written their names into West Ham's record books, and the different

club captains over the years. The process of actions needs to be well thought off, and it is no shame to consult the fans if you are unsure of what they want.

7. **Physical Evidence:** Almost all services include some physical elements, even if the bulk of what the consumer pays for is intangible. Showcasing what products and services the club can deliver adds credibility to the sales process. Of course, if not done right, the opposite effect may occur. For example, Manchester United FC is commercially the most advanced club in the world. However, some flaws can be seen in the marketing process. For example, a look at how they portray their hospitality formulas. The brochures are looking good, no? Well, this would be the perfect physical evidence of their different hospitality offerings if not the season 2016/2017 brochure was used to promote seasons 2019–2020.

In a football context, we can maybe add an 8P as well, *Prize*. You can be the best marketer there if your club is not winning prizes or not advancing properly in a sporting way; your campaigns will not reach extreme heights. It is unsurprising that winning major trophies will boost a fan base by as much as 200%.

# Brand marketing

Not every sale originates from the same driving force, but the goal is to ensure that both the current and future fan base perceive the brand in a positive light. Promotion of the brand in the football context would refer to the image or perceptions individuals have for a club and all assets attached to the club, for example, the players. Following a study in 2012 conducted by Kantar Media, Manchester United FC argued that they have 659 million followers worldwide (Ozanian, 2012). These include all individuals demonstrating positive associations with the club, even if they do not identify Manchester United as their favourite team (Beek, 2019). This number of individuals that form meaning for the club should be targeted; turning these followers into consumers is the next step. When looking at football clubs worldwide, some brands are more outspoken than others. The more outspoken the brand is positioned, the more straightforward a marketer can address its assets towards the fan base. There are two excellent examples: one can be found in Germany and the other in France.

# FC Sankt Pauli (FCSP)

FCSP occupies a distinctive position in world football. A bastion of left-wing activism and DIY (do-it-yourself) arts, its supporters, particularly the legendary 'ultras', are one of the western world's most politically and culturally engaged fanbases, and the club is particularly loved by punk and underground music fans. 'St Pauli is unlike any other club', says Tim McIlrath, frontman of American melodic hardcore band Rise Against. 'We went to their stadium and saw "No Football for Fascists" painted across the stand; seeing them encouraging more girls playing football – is fascinating. Looking for a club that transcends sport – St Pauli is a model of that' (Cartledge, 2018). This extract comes from an article published in 2018 by *The Guardian*. Technically speaking, FCSP is a football club from Germany located in the city of Hamburg. The truth is, it is way more than that. It is a lifestyle, an attitude. With a fan base that describes itself as left-wing punk rockers, the club makes a stand against fascism, racism, sexism, and homophobia. At the same time, it is the most Rock'n'Roll sports club in the world – AC/DC's "Hells Bells" blasting through the speakers when the team walks on. The association people have with the brand was not developed organically. For a club to reach this status, culture and history are not enough. Using the heritage by setting up live events, consistently communicating its values, and attracting its followers online is what the marketing department of FCSP did extremely well. As a result, the hype turns into a commercial advantage. Their clothing line embraces the rebellious spirit of the eponymous red-light district in Hamburg, coinciding with their brand-new American webshop; St Pauli brings its unique spirit across the ocean, endorsing several punk rock bands. All this is centralised on a designated website. With its integrated e-commerce platform, fans/customers can easily browse and buy the club's merchandise. Not bad for an organisation that calls itself 'non-commercial', right?

# Red Star Paris

Red Star FC (not to be confused with Red Star Belgrade)—over a century years old (France's second oldest) – directly opposes everything Paris Saint-Germain FC stands for. Red Star is unapologetically anti-corporate, rooted in social activism, and deeply connected with the working class.

Over the years, they have carved out their lane in culture for the club's strong association with local, national, and even international creative communities. As the club is based in the Seine-Saint-Denis district of Paris, an area with a long history of immigration from Africa and the Caribbean, diversity has always ensured the club's progress. It has inspired a creative outlook at every club level – also with whom they collaborate. Through co-branding, they are keeping their image up. Co-branding is an arrangement that associates a single product or service with more than one brand name or associates a product with someone other than the principal producer. Red Star FC's collaboration with Vice (progressive media organisation), Acid FC (design collective with disruption at its core), and WWWESH STUDIO (creative art collective) is the perfect example of this. In 2020, they combined their expertise to promote the club through fashion. The new shirts and their lifestyle collection represent what the club and its fan base stand for, creativity. The collection is considered the pet project of Red Star FC's creative director, ex-Manchester United striker David Bellion. Since taking up the role in 2016, Bellion has been instrumental in connecting Red Star FC and creative communities. Their fashion line is only one example. Another one? They recently launched a programme that sees the club's academy players participate in creative workshops after training.

These two examples show that the objectives of a football club are very different for each ownership model. Nevertheless, the marketing objectives regarding brand marketing are often very similar. Regardless of the chosen ownership model, each football club should aim to stay relevant to current and future fans and grow general interest in their brand.

> In an era of radical visibility, technology, and media, individuals are given the power to stand up for their opinions and beliefs on a grand scale. This power, reflected in everything from the #MeToo movement to the growing intolerance for 'fake news', is infiltrating every aspect of people's lives, including their purchasing decisions.
>
> (Accenture, 2018)

Companies, and even football clubs, are under the spotlight like never before as they struggle for competitive advantage in this reality. Where die-hard fans are emotionally very indifferent when it comes to off-the-pitch management, a large percentage of the overall consumers are emotionally more stable when it comes to expressing support. They are now assessing what a brand says, what it does, and what it stands for. A modern football enterprise should not take appreciation for granted. Playing into social awareness and using social marketing as a tool to get affection and support is becoming more and more important. Clubs should be aware of the importance of their message reaching all the entities and people that lend or may lend their support. Integrating corporate social responsibility (CSR) into strategic management can deliver several benefits that ultimately create and enhance a sustainable competitive advantage for the club. One of the world's biggest clubs realised this very early; FC Barcelona re-positioned themselves in light of the new international expansion plan. Compared to Real Madrid and Manchester United, they started targeting followers outside their country late. Because they did not have a first-mover advantage, they needed to design a proposal for supporters that was different from the rest. Two specific lines of positioning were set forward in the marketing strategy: charity and spectacular football. The formal phrasing looked like this: (Calzada, 2013) 'FC Barcelona (FCB) is the club most deeply committed to social causes; it drives social actions, with a particular focus on children, and it is at the service of its members'. Specifically, FCB has developed involvement activities as part of a broader CSR initiative, which was used to increase and maintain the bonds between the club and the international community. The following vehicles were used to help spread the word (Chanavat, 2017):

1. **Magazine:** A quarterly publication that provided information on prominent national and international projects. The Barca Foundation magazine is, at this point, still one of the best examples of how social marketing benefits brand perception.
2. **Online Newsletter:** A short, snappy content format informing on ongoing projects and reporting on the impact certain activities had on global communities.
3. **Annual Reports:** In cooperation with the main sponsor Beko, they provide a detailed record of the activities and projects developed by the Foundation.
4. **Publishing:** Books and articles provide the necessary physical evidence of the effect of their work.
5. **Foundation.fcbarcelona.com:** Designated websites with links to other activities offered by the club, Search Engine Optimisation done at the very highest level.

6. **Social Networks:** A strong presence on all social media channels to spread the word of their activities, the best PR you can have'.

One last example of how a clear marketing strategy can benefit a positive perception of the club by its followers is experiential marketing. Sports fans are simultaneously consumers and producers. Fans want to attend games, watch sports on television, talk about it in a bar over a glass of beer, and help to create the sport product. For example, a stadium without an excited crowd does not make for an existing contest (something we all experienced during the pandemic). Hence, customers are instrumental in helping to create tension, excitement, and atmosphere at a football game (UEFA). Furthermore, best of all, a football club can nurture this.

> Experiential marketing, also called 'engagement marketing', is a marketing strategy that invites an audience to interact with a business in a real-world situation. The business can show its customers what the company offers and what it stands for using participatory, hands-on, and tangible branding material.
>
> (Becker, 2021)

When an experiential marketing campaign is event-centric, it is dedicated less to the type of event – like a concert, festival, or conference – and more to interactions between the brand and the customer. Nevertheless, these campaigns must take an integrated approach.

> The primary purpose is to experience a brand in a tangible, offline way, but you will still want an online dialogue around it. Considering that 49% of folks create mobile videos at branded events – 39% of which are shared on Twitter – it makes sense to incorporate a digital element. A branded hashtag, for example, can get people talking about the experience.
>
> (Becker, 2021)

The best example in football is Dortmund's Yellow Wall,

> a spellbinding sight in the south stand of Borussia Dortmund's Signal Iduna Park that may not be quite visible from space, but whose dimensions and noise reach up to the stars. At 328ft long and 131ft

high, the Südtribüne, one of world football's most magnificent venue packs, are enough people to make up a town. A raucous, bellowing, spine-tingling town of Schwarzgelben souls that can cause opposing teams to wilt and BVB's best to bloom.

(Bundesliga, 2019)

Everybody wants to be there; everybody wants to experience this. The club did quite well in promoting this unique feeling. From regular posts on Instagram to crowd-inspired features on TikTok to interviews and testimonies from fans, every digital and social channel has been used to transfer a feeling of belonging to current and future fans. All these examples and strategies add up to increasing brand loyalty. Now, it is time to make some money.

# B2C marketing

B2C marketing or business-to-consumer marketing, refers to how a football club promotes its products and services to individuals. In a football club environment, B2C marketing is more or less part of the sales procedure (Harvey, sd). The products and services which can be sold to fans in this way are single tickets, season tickets, merchandising, club-licensed products, OTT platform subscriptions, food, beverages, non-matchday events, museum tickets, and membership schemes. Fans of football clubs are more likely to make impulse decisions; various factors can sway them and require trust to establish loyalty. However, it is worth noting that not all B2C prospects respond to the same marketing methods. Ultras would probably not be very much in favour of getting push notifications to buy various fan shop items; however, addressing families and younger fans with discounts on merchandising may have a positive effect on sales revenues. The right products can be linked with the right target group by relying on customer segmentation analysis (look at chapter 9, "Customer Relationship Management"). One of the best examples in recent years is the 2020/2021 kit launch campaign by Southampton FC:

The club has released an arcade-style video game, which takes players on a journey through its 135-year history to unlock the new home kit and mark the milestone year. Called 'Defying the Odds since 1885', a nod to the club's tenacious legacy, the video game features three levels for fans to conquer, each unlocking a different part of the new home kit once complete. Beginning in 1885 at the club's inception and leading up to the present day, the levels, which see the player donning consecutive historical kits, represent different eras in the club's history. The game's goal produced by 'Tech Company of the Year', UNIT9, is simple: dribble your way through history collecting as many points as possible by picking up various objects, avoiding obstacles, and 'defying the odds' along the way. The experience includes several hidden references that only true Saints and football fans will notice, including club cult heroes such as Matt Le Tissier, Kevin Keegan, Ali Dia, and Markus Liebherr taking a cue from the world of gaming. There are also various obstacles to avoid, including rival Portsmouth players, Liverpool's bank manager, and Harry Redknapp in his Range Rover. The game also includes notable sights: Southampton City landmarks, the old Wembley, where the club won the FA Cup in '76, Southampton's first stadium, the Dell, and the team's current home, St Mary's. Both Saints fans and football enthusiasts alike are sure to appreciate the game's level of detail and interactivity. Overall, winners on the live leaderboard stand a chance to win an ultimate football gaming bundle featuring a PS4 or Xbox and FIFA 2020. Runners-up can win a signed 20/21 replica shirt or a stadium tour with Matt Le Tissier.

(Southampton FC, sd)

The Southampton campaign is not an average marketing campaign. Many resources are poured into it by combining a specially designed app with targeted paid advertising to let it go viral. Football clubs can perfectly do fine without the bling-bling in their attempt to launch a brilliant push. Deploying data, well-planned timing, and clear communication of the club's value will go a long way. In 2018, the Liverpool Echo published an article on how Everton Football Club has registered a remarkable 17% increase in season ticket sales in the last two seasons – which, at best, could be described as ordinary (Liverpool Echo, 2018). Therefore, bad results on the pitch, but a rising number of people going to the Park. Furthermore, the Blues also boast a higher profile of younger fans than the rest of the league at their home games – 26% are 22 and under compared to 18% for the rest. How is that possible? Appropriately for a club known as the School of Science on the pitch, the sophistication and science involved off the pitch in achieving those figures are staggering. Some strategies are obvious. Everton's season ticket campaigns have become renowned for their emotive and engaging appeal. Videos and social media messages seek to reinforce Everton as not a potential family entertainment option but a ritual, an addiction, and part of the fabric of everyday life. There have been 'We go the game', 'It is in my heart', and 'Nothing will be the same' – campaigns that have seen Everton pick up accolades in, for example, the Football Business Awards. A great example of using emotion in campaigns is the poem called Home, crafted by National Football Museum's Poet in Residence and Everton fan Paul Cookson. The poem was the starting point for the season ticket rally and perfectly encapsulates what coming to Goodison is all about. Coming to the game is something Evertonians are rightly proud of. Taking that pride and using Paul's words alongside some of the visual representations of fans in the stands at Goodison and taking part in their rituals before the game really captures the essence of Everton at 'home'. Everton FC presented the poem in a video so it can be shared easily by fans – and focussed on fans getting involved by telling their stories and rituals so the club can showcase these to other fans in the months after the launch. However, the ticket sales increased not only owing to the poem. The analytics behind it turned the season ticket campaign into a measurable success. The Blues focussed on 'at risk' fans, meaning, Everton officials seek to find out why a season ticket holder misses two or more matches by calling them personally.

The club will seek to put supporters in touch with other fans from similar areas of the country to create a greater match-going experience if a supporter regularly travels a long distance to watch home matches. Everton has calculated that less than 4% of fans stop coming if they have been regulars for five years or more. Therefore, they have targeted new season ticket holders and have seen first-year retention rise from 73% to 83%. A 12-point algorithm was then employed to try and retain season ticket holders once the matchday experience has hooked them.

To again highlight the importance of data when it comes to getting to know fans and delivering meaningful marketing activities, we will give another example of a season ticket sales process done right; the 2017/2018 season ticket campaign of Aston Villa FC revolved around '#MyVillaMoments' and included the combination of various live data sources to create a progressive, fully personalised, and responsive website for every season ticket holder and match ticket purchaser. The personalised URL (address of a webpage) allowed them to re-live the defining moments of the 16/17 season – to truly see what they would be missing without a season ticket in 17/18. Using rich media, behavioural data, and Opta stats, they created over 50,000 websites with 19 variable data sources in each. The campaign goal was to build a 1-to-1 conversation with their supporters, highlighting the exciting moments of their attendance at Villa Park to encourage season ticket renewal or purchase. Other aims included a target of early bird sales, a specific marketing return on investment (ROI), a % renewal rate, and a set revenue vs. several season ticket holders. The campaign was the most successful season ticket marketing campaign in the past ten years, breaking several records and all targets, despite the club finishing in its lowest position for 44 years (Football Business Awards, 2018).

# B2B marketing

As the name suggests, business-to-business marketing refers to marketing products or services to other businesses and organisations. In a broad sense, B2B marketing content is more informational and straightforward than B2C. This is because business purchase decisions, compared to those of consumers, are based more on bottom-line revenue impact. ROI is rarely a consideration for the everyday person – at least in a monetary sense – but it is a primary focus for corporate decision-makers (Harvey, Planning your B2B marketing strategy, sd). The products and services that can be sold to businesses are corporate boxes, corporate area utilisation, commercial floor space, sponsorship and partnership schemes, business club memberships, media rights, and marketing services. In this case, the marketing department's role is the promotion of the offerings to other businesses and brands. Although the activations of partnerships should be part of the B2B marketing strategy, we will not discuss this in this chapter. For more information on how co-branding activities and partnership or sponsorship activations can be realised, look at chapter 15, "Partnership and Sponsorship."

As stated before, supporting the sales process of B2B offerings is one of the key responsibilities of the club's marketing team. As sponsorship and partnership revenue can make up to 30% of a club's total revenue, it would be unwise not to focus on this aspect within the marketing strategy. One of the easiest ways of supporting partnership and sponsorship acquisition is by showcasing successful collaborations with other brands and businesses. LinkedIn is the perfect medium to portray these best practices. A small

Belgian club, KV Kortrijk, brilliantly did this. At the end of the 2018/2019 season, they published a whitepaper on the effect of partnering up with their football club. Explaining how they activate and support a partnership with real-life facts and figures gave extra visibility to their current partners. They grasped the attention of other brands looking into sports sponsorship. On a larger scale, Olympique Lyonnais has also deployed this strategy. They actively share all business activities of the club on their different media channels, an overview of the yearly activities lined up for the members of the business club, impact studies on partnerships, and sponsorship showcase content.

Digital marketing plays a huge part in selling business features like corporate boxes, corporate area utilisation, and commercial floor space renting. Corporate clients and other businesses need to know what a club can offer before they consider engaging in a formal agreement. SEO, SEM (Search Engine Marketing), social media, and content marketing are extremely important to boost the digital campaign. The effect of social media to increase brand and product awareness and how content marketing can be used in searching for other partnerships have already been discussed. No word has been said about SEO and SEA (Search Engine Advertising) as tools for actively promoting the club's offerings (in this case, from a B2B perspective but also perfectly transferable to B2C marketing). SEO stands for 'search engine optimisation'. Simply, it means improving the site's visibility for relevant searches. The more visible the pages are in search results, the more likely you are to garner attention and attract prospective and existing customers to your club's offering (Goodwin, sd). SEO is a fundamental part of digital marketing because people conduct trillions of searches yearly, often with commercial intent to find information about products and services. Greater visibility and ranking higher in search results than the competition can have a material impact on your bottom line. Optimising the search results to attract more attention to a club's B2B offerings can be done in various ways. One of them is by displaying offerings by using relevant search terms. Want to attract business events to the stadium? Use relevant tag lines related to the hospitality and event sector. Want to rent out floor space for commercial use? Try to look up how the real estate sector promotes its services. A more proactive way of advertising these services can be done with SEA. Search engine advertising (also known as search advertising, internet search advertising, or online search advertising) allows you to directly display your paid ads among the search results on various search engines, like

Google, Bing, and Yahoo. Advertisers who utilise search advertising show their ads to users actively searching for specific keywords and pay a fee every time someone clicks on the ad. This PPC (pay-per-click) advertising is especially effective because people who conduct searches tend to reveal their intent with their search query. Operating a stadium in a certain region where you know commercial event space is limited? Advertising in this way can boost the infrastructure to become top of mind for businesses looking to host their events at an external venue. One of the leading companies assisting football clubs in reaching their B2B goals is SportFive (the former Lagardère Sports). For years, they have been the go-to agency for brands and media platforms wanting to collaborate with rights holders worldwide to reach emotionally engaged audiences; for smaller football organisations, engaging with these kinds of agencies to promote products and services and drive sales can be of great value. An example of a club relying on the services offered by SportFive in relation to their stadium operation services is Ferencvaros TC. In 2014, SportFive signed a minimum ten-year stadium operation and club marketing contract with the Hungarian 28-times record champions from Budapest. The deal encompasses the whole operation, management, and marketing of the stadium, including the naming right as well as comprehensive marketing rights of the club.

# Measuring impact

Defining the ROI when it comes to marketing is challenging. Until now, no club or agency has found the magic formula to conduct an audit on direct revenues generated through certain go-to-market activities. It is best to analyse the activities ad-hoc per campaign to measure the impact of marketing activities. To measure impact and evaluate the efforts, having relevant data is uttermost important. As told by Fiona Green in her book *Winning with Data*, one of the many benefits of marketing in the digital world is the ability to test theories or ideas before committing to them. Consider the process of printing a poster to promote ticket sales. The design is produced based on all the information available at the time. Show it around to colleagues in the office and maybe to a few other people whose opinions are respected. Then, order 100, 1,000, or 10,000 of them and have them printed. At this point, you are committed. The poster includes an offer code, so ROI can be tracked when the fans book their tickets. However, what is not known is the conversion rate; how many people saw the poster and then went on to use the code? Furthermore, it is unknown how much the conversion rate would have increased had the wording or imagery been different, if the posters had been placed in different positions, or on a different day. Compare that with the process of producing, for example, email campaigns, banner ads, a landing page, or, indeed, any piece of digital content. In any of these instances, while again producing the digital asset based on the information gotten at the time, by using a testing process, the amendment can be done based on the information gathered as the customers engage with it. In many instances, the process can be automated for added efficiency. When testing is used, an informed decision is made based on an objective, non-subjective, data-driven process. The chances of making an incredible breakthrough and implementing a bad idea will be reduced (Green, 2021).

A crucial piece of advice we can give: analyse, test, and re-target. The impact can be measured by gathering intelligence and applying this to the set objectives at the start. Want to reach a wider audience? Analyse the different platforms to reach fans, measure the effectiveness of the content strategy, look for opportunities on existing channels, and ask yourself if new technology opportunities could help along the way. Want to optimise digital platforms by improving the content delivered? Have a look at the conversion rate optimisation and the traffic sources, use personal user journeys to align the needs of the consumer with the digital offerings, measure the impact of the SEO and SEA strategy, and try to find out if there is a change in the likely-to-buy behaviour of the fans. Looking to improve data collection to build data records? Analyse how to collect data from all points of sales, see if individual staff targets in data collection per department are met, analyse the working tools, and measure the impact of incentives to convince fans to hand over their data.

# City dressing

Marketing is about reaching the target groups online and offline and communicating messages clearly. One of the oldest forms of marketing is hanging posters all over the city to raise the visibility of the message. Now, when everything is about social media, the traditional ways of marketing are often forgotten. Nevertheless, posters in the city have been replaced by digital billboards, public transport can be wrapped, and flags are always a good way to dress a city centre. The point that I want to make is that there is no excuse that someone can drive or walk around in the city centre where a football club is located for hours without seeing the club logo or slogan or hearing its chant. Good examples of city dressing are FC Barcelona and Real Madrid. Their digital posters announcing the next home match are always present in the city, as fans hang flags outside their window to show their support for the club. Manchester City FC uses city billboards to activate several big moments, such as the announcement of their new club badge or the arrival of a new player. A city benefits from attraction and gains name recognition when a football club performs. Therefore, a city should breathe football, and the club should be as visible as possible. It will also remind citizens of upcoming matches if communication is on point.

## Key takeaways

- Ask the three questions of marketing to evaluate previous campaigns.
- Do not be arrogant, thinking everybody should automatically be interested in the club.
- The priority is to create attraction towards the club.
- Implement the 7 Ps of marketing.
- Sporting results can be an accelerator and have a huge impact; nevertheless, the brand identity, positioning, and values should be clear first to maximise the acceleration.
- Dare to stand out and be unique.
- Go digital but do not forget that offline marketing can still be very powerful.
- Claim the city and make it breathe football.

## References

Accenture. (2018). *To Affinity and Beyond*. Accenture.

American Marketing Association. (2017). *Definition of Marketing*. Retrieved from ama.org: https://www.ama.org/the-definition-of-marketing-what-is-marketing/

Becker, B. (2021, August 16). *Best Experiential Marketing Campaigns*. Retrieved from Hubspot: https://blog.hubspot.com/marketing/best-experiential-marketing-campaigns

Beek, E. V. (2019). Global Football: Defining the Rules of the Changing Game. In D. P. Simon Chadwick, *Routledge Handbook of Football Business and Management* (pp. 90–91). Taylor & Francis.

Bundesliga. (2019, February 14). *Yellow Wall*. Retrieved from Bundeslige: https://www.bundesliga.com/en/bundesliga/news/yellow-wall-wiki-borussia-dortmund-signal-iduna-park-bvb-3357-2391

Calzada, E. (2013). *Show Me the Money!* (p.35).Bloomsbury.

Cartledge, L. (2018, June). *FC St Pauli: How It Became the Football Team of Punk and Techno*. Retrieved from The Guardian: https://www.theguardian.com/music/2018/jun/20/fc-st-pauli-how-it-became-the-football-team-of-punk-and-techno

Chanavat, N., Desbordes, M., & Lorgnier, N. (Eds.). (2017). *Routledge Handbook of Football Marketing* (p. 301). Taylor & Francis.

Derby County FC. (2012, July 27). *Demand Ticket Pricing explained*. Retrieved from dcfc: https://www.dcfc.co.uk/news/2012/07/demand-ticket-pricing-explained

Football Business Awards. (2018). *Best Marketing Initiative*. Retrieved from football-businessawards: https://footballbusinessawards.com/winner/best-club-marketing-initiative-non-premier-league-2017/

Goodwin, D. (sd). *What Is SEO*. Retrieved from Search engine land: https://search-engineland.com/guide/what-is-seo

Green, F. (2021). *Winning with Data* (pp. 110–111). Taylor & Francis.

Harvey, S. (sd). *Planning Your B2B Marketing Strategy*. Retrieved from Fabrik Brands: https://fabrikbrands.com/planning-your-b2b-marketing-strategy/

Harvey, S. (sd). *The Essential Guide for B2C Marketing*. Retrieved from Fabrik Brands: https://fabrikbrands.com/the-essential-guide-for-b2c-marketing/

Liverpool Echo. (2018, April). *Everton Season Tickets*. Retrieved from liverpoolecho: https://www.liverpoolecho.co.uk/sport/football/football-news/everton-season-tickets-more-popular-14534823

Ozanian, M. (2012, May 29). Retrieved from forbes.com: https://www.forbes.com/sites/mikeozanian/2012/05/29/manchester-united-claims-to-have-659-million-supporters/

Southampton FC. (2021). Retrieved from Southamptonfc: https://www.southamptonfc.com/official-replica-kit-20-21

UEFA. (2021). In *Handbook of Football Association Management* (p. 119). UEFA.

# 14 Communication management

We look back to the brand identification and positioning to set up a proper communication plan. Having earlier defined what the brand is standing for and the reason for its existence, we can now create a communication plan based on the marketing KPIs.

No matter the country or league your football club plays in, the club is always trying to become a love brand for its fans. The three primary factors of a love brand are:

1. **Mystery:** does the brand tell a story? Does the story inspire the consumer and even tempt them to dream?
2. **Sensuality:** can the brand be experienced with the senses? Does it have its own sound, a distinct look, or a certain feeling?
3. **Intimacy:** Can the customer build an emotional relationship with the brand through empathy, passion, and dedication?

There are six steps in creating the perfect communication plan for your football club (Table 14.1).

1. The first one is defining the business objectives. What does the club want to accomplish through their communication? Driving sales, being informative, creating a buzz, being top of mind, press relations, CSR (Corporate Social Responsibility), or lead generation? If you have multiple objectives, create multiple communication plans.
2. In the second step, we ensure that the football club has social governance, objectives, and KPIs in place. This means that it is important that the drive for content creation and becoming a social company is being

DOI: 10.4324/9781003312680-17

Table 14.1 The Social Media Lasagna (Courtesy of Vinckier, 2017)

| Business Objectives | | |
|---|---|---|
| Social Objectives & KPIs | | |
| Target Audience | | |
| Content | | |
| Channels | Sender | Form |
| Tactics | | |

pushed from or supported by the management of a football club. Access to players, dressing rooms, and trainings is crucial, and the coach or sporting director often misunderstands the importance of social media. Nevertheless, the focus should not always be on the players and the sporting results. A football club has so many other stories to tell.

3. Once you have defined the objectives, it is time to set the target audience. Different objectives may have different target audiences. Therefor it is important to adapt your communication accordingly while keeping the same brand identity.

4. After you have set your target audience, you need to select your communication channels accordingly. Ensure that you know which channels your target audiences are using. As nowadays everyone is focussing on online media, do not forget the communication possibilities through offline media such as newspapers, billboards, and magazines.

5. Content is King! Creating unique and engaging content has become so important in the past decade. Social media channels have an important role in the life of teenagers and almost all groups in society. Remember that each channel requires a different content strategy. Do not just talk about your product; remember your 'why', which has been discussed earlier.

6. Now that you are all set up, it is important to grow your channels and gain as much reach, followers, and engagement as possible. Will you use paid advertising or focus on organic growth? Smart tactics will help to become successful on social media.

# Content is king

Eight out of ten posts on social media should not be about your product! But what else should you post about? Social media is a long-term strategy, and will not generate revenues a week after setting up your accounts. It is one of the many reasons why 'old-school' directors are not a fan of social media. Football club directors have said 'Content creation is expensive and time-consuming. It takes the focus away from the players, and there is always a risk for a post to backfire'. And also, 'By selling one player, the club generates as much revenue as social media would generate in a decade'. Now that fan attendances were dropping after the COVID pandemic, those directors are probably wondering why their fans are not as engaged anymore.

As social media already exists for over a decade, I will not explain what it is or how it works. However, I will explain how football clubs can use social media to build a relationship with their fans, expand that fan base, and develop the brand towards a love brand. The key that can open all those doors is twofold. Content creation will be super important, but excellent content is still worthless without a story. Reflect on the exercise you did while defining the club's brand identity. Now that you have the club's 'Why' in mind, think about what football clubs can share about the following topics:

- Nostalgia
- Local content
- Human stories
- Behind the scenes
- News
- Corporate Communication
- Expertise
- Fashion
- Top Topical
- Partners & sponsors

Focus on finding the content sweet spot and the disproportionate relevance between the football club and your target group. Finding the balance between rational and emotional posts, focussing on creating awareness, research/data, comparisons, and purchases is important, but it also opens many possibilities.

Knowing how to use your social media channels and what content to use on which platform is crucial in your communication. Often, we see football clubs using the same content on all their different platforms. This is a bad

Table 14.2 Difference between Twitter and Facebook

| Twitter | | Facebook | |
|---------|---|----------|---|
| Breaking news | Announce news as soon as it happens | Regularity | Post 5–10 times a day |
| | | | Consistent matchday, and non-matchday schedules |
| Rich media | Multi photo & video tweets | Engagement | Tailor content to drive commenting. |
| | | | Use voting, questions, competitions |
| Amplify yourself | Tag players, clubs, competitions, join popular conversations | Algorithm | Approximate rule: total engagement x total reach/#posts |
| Value others | Reply, retweet, follow, favourite, ask questions … | Content | Video's – status updates have the furthest reach |
| Exclusive access | Tweet behind the scenes features | Authentic voice | Less formal than website |

strategy as fans will go from following all social media channels to one channel. As an example, find hereunder the difference between Twitter and Facebook (Table 14.2).

Know that you do not always need to generate new content or make content yourself. There are four different content types to share:

1. **Created content:** Our own created content
2. **Curated content:** Content created by someone else and shared on your own media
3. **Repurposed content:** Re-used content that you already had but used in a slightly different way
4. **Co-created content:** Content created with a sponsor or with your audience

# Visual identity

If someone who is not a football fan sees a social media post without the brand name or logo, that person should still be able to recognise which football club is communicating. It is all about being consistent in the way the club communicates. Define the proper form of your message and the right tone of voice. Should the tone be formal or informal? Serious or funny? Mature or youthful? Technical or accessible? Institutional or personal?

Of course, the tone of voice can differ for each platform depending on the target group you're trying to reach. Apart from a voice tone, colours, and other visuals are also important to create a visual identity.

# The Egyptian effect

Numbers do not always reveal everything. Put numbers in perspective when you analyse them. In football, transfers often greatly impact increasing social media followers. We call this 'the Egyptian effect'. There are numerous examples of where social media followers grew exceptionally after a transfer. Juventus gained around 6 million followers after the announcement of Cristiano Ronaldo, and PSG gained approximately 10 million followers after they announced Lionel Messi. And even smaller clubs benefit from transfers. Will those followers stay connected to the club and spend money on merchandise and ticketing? We are not convinced about that, but these numbers are important for global sponsors. After Ronaldo left Manchester United to go to Saudi Arabian side Al Nassr the impact on social media was enormous. Their Instagram followers went through the roof from 853.000 to 13.1 million (on 20th February 2023). The announcement post received 34.594.054 likes. Al Nassr has now more Instagram followers than big European clubs such as AS Roma (5.4m), Inter (8.9m), Sevilla FC (2m), and Olympique de Marseille (2,8m).

# Timing

Another important factor is knowing when to communicate. Fans want to receive updates from the club as much as possible. They want to know what's happening at the club, how the players are doing, possible transfers, and match preparations. Every day there must be communication between the fans and the club. Not just once a day like many clubs do. If you want to build a community, communication is crucial. But what is the ideal timing to communicate? Hereunder, we can see an example that FC Bayern München uses in their social media strategy (Steen, 2018).

The everyday communication:
07:00 – Breaking news through the mobile club app
08:00 – Social media check -> post on FB, twitter, LinkedIn, Instagram, …

08:30 – Fans listen to the club podcast

01:00 pm – Lunch break means watching club TV

04:00 pm – Fans check their e-mails = club newsletter

06:00 pm – On the way home = social media check

08:00 pm – Home surfing on laptop = website/web-shop promotions

Schedule your social media posts according to the average daily schedule of your fans. Each social network has its specific features and is very different from each other at which time the customers are using them. Build your strategy accordingly.

# Campaigns

After analysing which media channels or communication methods are preferred by the fans, and the ideal timings of your daily communication, the development of a campaign can begin. Use your club's brand and its audience to be an influencer and to bring the right products from the club's partners to the right target groups by using CRM (Customer Relationship Management).

Different campaigns can be:

- **Email campaigns**
  - Blueprint
  - Ticket alert
  - Post-match
  - Community focussed
- **Automated campaigns**
  - Birthday email
  - If a season ticket holder (STH) misses a match
  - When a season ticket holder (STH) comes for X-games
- **Ticketing campaigns**
  - Special email campaign for the start of season ticket sales and single tickets

Each campaign has a fixed cycle, and follows the same steps (Figure 14.1).

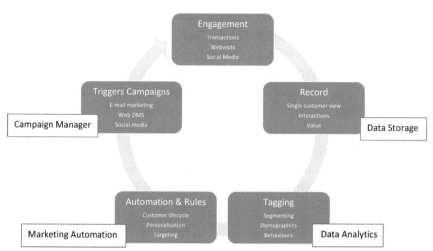

*Figure 14.1* Digital marketing campaign cycle. (Courtesy of Borges, 2017.)

# Sponsorship value

The value of sponsorship can be greatly enhanced through effective communication. By utilising the various communication channels available to clubs, they can increase their visibility and engage with fans. This can be achieved through various means, such as publishing editorials on the club's website or app, sending marketing emails via the club's CRM system, collaborating on social media content, and promoting membership programs or e-gaming.

# Social media is not free

A non-written rule is that 20% of your marketing budget should be allocated to digital marketing. Boardroom members often inquire about the return on investment (ROI) of social media. If you compare a Facebook or Instagram boosted post with a magazine ad, the impressions reached can be very similar, but the cost for the boosted post will be way less than the magazine advertisement. We highly recommend football clubs to work with influencers to reach the best results. Why? The power is in the network of the people. When a football club shares content on their social media page, they have a 3% organic reach from the total amount of followers. The peers reach per brand ambassador is much higher. Football clubs often create links with famous stars such as Rafael Nadal, a huge Real Madrid fan or Idris Elba, a big Arsenal fan (Vinckier, 2017).

So, what is the ROI of social media?

It is cost-effective, measurable, scalable, and easy to convert. Many football clubs are still not using paid advertisements because they believe they are the biggest football club in the area and that fans should follow them anyway. Yet they keep complaining about the decline of stadium attendances and season card holders.

Football clubs are often running behind on trends and implementing new ways of doing business. Social media is not a toy anymore and it is not only for marketing purposes. It is time that football clubs become a social company. This means that there is a vision shared by all, a social strategy, governance, departments, and ambassadors in place. One of the most important steps in becoming a social company is giving your social media team the mandate to post updates, react without asking permission, boost or advertise posts, show behind the scenes, have access to players, staff, changing room and have access to the website and analytics.

# Social crisis plan

Although it might never happen, you better prepare to make sure the club's ready when shit hits the fan. Make a list of possible situations and categorise them based on a crisis level. For instance, level one crisis could be: Bad customer service, and level 5 could be an unforeseen disaster. List under each level a few examples, which employees are involved, when and where to reply, and most importantly, how to apply.

# 7 Cs of social media

Nick Vinckier explained the best social media strategy in seven easy steps (Vinckier, 2017).

Start by capturing your stakeholders. This can be done through the following:

a. Educate the market
b. Initiate – buzz – Guerilla marketing
c. Create awareness for the full product range
d. Remain top of mind

After having captured your stakeholders, convince them to follow your football club. This can be achieved by following the steps hereunder.

a. Create a proper brand image
b. Change public perception
c. Humanisation/show DNA/be transparent
d. Create thought leadership
e. Personal brands as a lever

When stakeholders are convinced to follow the football club's social media channels, it is time to convert them into customers.

a. Quality lead generation
b. Social Selling
c. Direct online revenue (e-commerce; online sales)
d. Omnichannel conversion: online promotion for offline purchases
e. Social recruiting employer branding + targeting

All the club's stakeholders are key in the club's environment. You will keep your stakeholders attached to your brand by caring for them.

a. Conversation management
b. Customer care
c. After-sales support
d. Online crisis management

Despite what many believe, social media is not a one-way direction. Collaborating with your stakeholders will tighten the relationship and open opportunities.

a. Community management
b. Loyalty & retention
c. Keep former players on track after they leave
d. Ambassadorship
e. Influencers marketing

Communicate, communicate, and communicate. I cannot express enough how important it is to talk to your stakeholders. Explain difficult situations they might not understand as they do not have all the information. Fan protests cannot always be avoided, but clear communication will help to ease the fans.

a.  Internal communication
b.  Press relations
c.  CSR
d.  Government & union communication
e.  Financial communication: stakeholders and investors

Finally, social media is often the 'Wild West'. As a football club, you should have certain policies to control your stakeholders and set boundaries. This can be about racism and bullying, but also positive things should be controlled.

a.  Customer validation of new products/new markets
b.  Employee policy
c.  Trends & competition watching
d.  Conversation monitoring
e.  Opportunity spotting
f.  Learning from results & data

## Comparison

Regarding popularity on social media, LaLiga and the Premier League are miles ahead of all the other leagues. The Premier League leads the way on Instagram with 64 million followers in February 2023, and LaLiga has the most followers on Facebook with 77 million likes in February 2023. Social media followers and engagement are key indicators for clubs and leagues' global and local footprints. Social Media and the data that comes with it have become a very important factor in overall football club valuation and the determination of the value of sponsorship contracts.

# Revenue through communication

Smaller football clubs do not often have the financial resources to invest heavily in a communication team. Big clubs such as Real Madrid – Manchester City have over 30 people working in their communication departments. For smaller clubs, a good way to grow would be to invest in or acquire a communication agency to have a full-time team available but not at expensive costs.

On the one hand, by acquiring an agency or starting a new business, the wages and heavy costs for cameras and other products do not fall on a football club's expenses. But more importantly, on the other hand, a communication agency is easier to market and create an income stream than a communication department of a football club.

Some football clubs are already experimenting with this but not yet in the right atmosphere. For instance: Ferencvarosi created the company 'Fradi Media' as their communication agency with platforms such as FRADI TV, a special website, and magazines. However, the brand 'Fradi Media' has too much link with the football club Ferencvarosi (Fradi is the club's nickname). We see a similar example with 'Club Media' from Belgian football club Club Brugge FC and 'Inter Media' for football club Internazionale.

We advise separating the brand of the communication agency from the brand of the football club but communicating the cooperation to all stakeholders. The football club can easily connect sponsors and partners to the communication agency. It can give access to expensive marketing channels through their visibility assets such as LED screens and social media. By doing so, the communication agency will become self-sustainable in no time and become a source of revenue for the football club instead of being a cost. In addition, you have a fully dedicated, experienced agency handling your communication for a less cost.

## Key takeaways

- Have a unique visual identity that matches the brand identity.
- Define the digital strategy of the club and act accordingly.
- As algorithms are changing from time to time, it's important to keep on learning.

- Don't think that social media is free, set a budget matching the objectives.
- Be creative when you don't have the necessary budgets available.
- Follow the 7 Cs of social media.

# References

Borges, C. (2017). *Digital Marketing Campaign Cycle*. Brussels: Manchester City FC.

Steen, B. (2018). *Communication Schedule Bayern München*. Brussels: Bayern München.

Vinckier, N. (2017). *Creating a Communication Plan*. Duval Union Consulting.

# Partnership and sponsorship

## 15

### Simon Van Kerckhoven and Martijn Ernest

Let me clarify that sponsorship and partnership are distinct concepts, despite their frequent intermingling. Sponsorship involves the purchase of advertising space at a football club, such as LED displays, social media posts, billboards, and jersey logos, in exchange for payment. In contrast, a partnership between a brand and a football club entails a deeper and more sustainable connection, with a duration of at least three years, often longer, and built on trust and collaboration towards shared goals.

Previously, football clubs employed concessionaires or intermediaries to maximise their sponsorship revenues. While intermediaries add value in an opaque marketplace, well-structured clubs have limited need for them. Direct dealings between clubs and sponsors offer value on an emotional level and in transparency, openness, and mutual understanding. Football clubs have developed sponsorship departments to facilitate these relationships, implemented sales strategies and support systems, and hired sales specialists with relevant skills or training to go to market. Effective communication requires understanding the targeted brand's plans, objectives, and metrics and investing in research to provide personalised proposals to targeted audiences. In addition to marketing, football clubs require capable sales specialists, sophisticated presentations, business intelligence, and customer marketing capabilities or resources.

An example of a successful sponsorship pitch is Chelsea FC's strategy of sending personalised, football-themed cases to top CEOs of the world's largest companies. These cases contained a customised shirt, a Premier League winner medal, and a video tailored to each company. The video showed the CEOs' life if they became Chelsea FC's sponsor, with every detail personalised to the recipient company. This pitch resulted in a bidding war and a £40 million per year deal with Yokohama.

DOI: 10.4324/9781003312680-18

Sponsorship is a substantial source of revenue for football clubs, accounting for between 20% and 35% of total commercial revenues on average. These revenues have grown substantially over the past few decades, with yearly increases. While a football club's sporting performance, global reach, and fan recognition may impact revenue growth, as evidenced by Manchester United's commercial success, these factors are not the sole determinants.

# Sponsorship types

Four main types of sponsorship are relevant for football clubs.

1. **Technical sponsorship:** Businesses provide access to products or services the football club needs. Often there is a benefit in kind for the football club.
2. **Commercial sponsorship:** Private brands that enter a commercial relationship with the football club.
3. **Institutional sponsorship:** Funding is linked to local or national government institutions.
4. **Ownership sponsorship:** The business of the club owner provides funding to the club through a sponsorship package.

# Sponsorship agreements

A sponsorship agreement has multiple elements to discuss before closing the agreement. As at the start of every relationship, it is important to be on the same page, and therefore have discussed the following topics:

- Exclusivity
- Duration
- Geographical area
- Sponsorship rights
- Sponsorship fee
- Renewal rights
- Post-termination

- Sponsorship evaluation
- Communication

# Sponsorship rights

The number of sponsorable assets at a football club is enormous. Football clubs need to realise the possible assets that are interesting for brands. Vice versa, brands need to know the possibilities at football clubs either. There has been a huge shift in the most valuable assets for brands. A decade ago, this used to be visibility and fan engagement, but data has become a big new asset for football clubs. As a football club, you better have your CRM system ready. An example was the latest deal between Spotify and FC Barcelona, where FC Barcelona's data greatly impacted the sponsorship value of the deal, as Spotify was looking for first-person data.

For football clubs with an international reach, new technologies such as digital overlay techniques on LED screens have become a game-changing reality. Football clubs can develop regional rights and assets in each category with this new technology.

However, the real value for a sponsor comes from the story they are telling together. It is all about making the partnership come alive. One of the best examples in recent years has been the partnership between Benfica CF and Emirates. Their partnership video has been watched millions of times on YouTube and was so successful that Emirates repeated the same activation at other clubs they sponsor. Partnership is much more than a billboard with a brand logo.

Exclusivity is the basis for a strong relationship. Special titles such as Official Airline or Official Furniture Partner are a good next step and give additional value to the partnership. Providing a rationale for the collaboration, such as product placement or multiple activation platforms, are even better. Nonetheless, the sweet spot is to expand the relationship with value-in-kind aspects that can be activated and communicated to the fans.

It is a challenge to offer all the above in tailor-made packages to potential sponsors. If football clubs do not have research teams, I recommend starting from a standard package and adding the flexibility to tailor it to the sponsor's needs. Listen to their marketing and sales strategy to discover their objectives, target groups, and current strategy to reach their objectives. However, it is perfectly possible for sponsorship not to have a marketing & sales purpose but maybe a public relationship or employee recruitment or rewarding purpose.

# Sponsorship pricing

Maintaining consistency in sponsorship pricing can be complex. A sponsorship rights inventory system is a key tool to define which assets are limited to which sponsorship category. An inventory system or application can help football clubs to develop quickly and price packages consistently, decide on discounts, and maximise the sale of all available assets. It also enables clubs to go the extra mile by adding an asset that has not been sold and giving it as an extra to overdeliver and maintain long-term relationships.

In recent years, a new sponsorship trend has emerged, which involves adding variable components to the contract at the request of sponsors. While many of these contracts include bonuses for sporting results, such performance-based criteria can pose financial risks to football clubs during underperformance. Instead of focussing solely on sporting results, aiming at value drivers such as digital fans, stadium attendance, and engagement rates is preferable.

A well-defined sponsorship category structure can be a good indication to decide which rights to allocate to which package. As economic situations vary by country, examining a benchmark report before allocating prices to different sponsorship categories is recommended. Collaborating closely with the club's Chief Financial Officer and Commercial Director can help decide on reasonable sponsorship revenue targets. The higher the category of sponsorship, the more exclusive the package becomes, and the higher the investment for brands will be.

# Sponsorship pyramid structure

Football clubs often see a sponsorship pyramid structure to categorise sponsors based on revenue value. The club can allocate certain assets and sponsorship rights in each category through the structure. For example, the stadium naming rights will only be available for a club's main partner, and fixed boarding at the youth academy might only be available for a regional or official club partner. Each club decides how they structure its sponsorship pyramid and the valuation they allocate to each asset. Hereunder, you can find a fictional example (Figure 15.1 and Table 15.1).

*Figure 15.1* Sponsorship pyramid structure

*Table 15.1* Sponsorship Pyramid Valuation Structure

| Target Fee | # Positions | Media Value | Structure Place |
|---|---|---|---|
| + €5m | 2–3 | €21m | Main Partner |
| + €2m | 5 | €13m | Global Partner |
| + €1m | 8 | €5m | Official Partner |
| €200K | 4/region | €500K | Regional Partner |

# Sponsorship relationships

In a successful sponsorship relationship, both parties are willing to go above and beyond for each other. However, football clubs need to provide a return on investment (ROI) report to their main sponsorship partners. This report justifies the investment and includes data and numbers, such as audience and media value. Clubs can evaluate sponsorship activations and other package elements to enhance the report. In addition, measuring sponsorship awareness through a survey and checking if the brand perception has changed during the sponsorship duration can be helpful. There are many suppliers available to assist with these reports.

In business and personal relationships, communication is key. Scheduling regular meetings to review data and qualitative results, discuss improvements, and making plans is crucial. Clubs should provide a clear overview of which rights or assets the sponsor has yet to use and help

| Partner | Custom Partnership Package | Football Club |
|---|---|---|
| **Marketing & Sales Strategy** | | **Inventory of Rights & Benefits** |

Planning / Evaluation / Creative development / Execution & Activation

*Figure 15.2* Partnership process. (Courtesy of AC Milan, 2018b.)

them to exploit all rights in the best way possible. Honesty is always the best policy for a long-term relationship, and ensuring the sponsor is happy and utilising all the rights they paid for is essential. If a certain asset is not meeting expectations, it should be communicated, and a solution proposed to the sponsor.

Interaction between the club's sponsorship employees and the brand directors on B2B occasions is also vital. It strengthens the relationship between the club and sponsor and allows other partners to know each other. Social events allow the explanation of business cases around certain themes and networking.

All the above components are what make a successful partnership. The term is often overused, but true partnerships are proven to hold the most value, as demonstrated by AC Milan. Despite several difficult sporting seasons, the club maintained high attractiveness to other brands, with multiple partnerships lasting over decades, such as Emirates, Audi, Dolce & Gabbana, Technogym, and Nivea. By becoming champions of Italy again after 11 years and generating massive international exposure, the loyalty of those brands was proven to be worthwhile.

A partnership process involves offering a partnership package of marketing instruments that best meet the brand's marketing and sales strategy. During each season, planning, implementing, and evaluating all activities and assets using research and data analytics are important steps to building a trusted environment (Figure 15.2).

# Partnership pillars

There are six partnership pillars to create a fruitful relationship (Table 15.2).

149

Table 15.2 Partnership Pillars (Courtesy of AC Milan, 2018a)

| Brand association | Visibility | Experiences |
|---|---|---|
| As a brand, this means the right to be publicly linked to the football club and benefit from the interest it generates and the value it represents. The main tools are a logo + description, partnership video, and images. | The right to obtain brand visibility through positioning the partner's brand in the context of the football club. This can be during home matches in the stadium or on television through interview backdrops, media channels and other tools such as institutional materials. | The right to offer exclusive experiences to a partner's key relation at matches or other club occasions. This can be match experiences such as visiting the dressing room, a meet & greet with a player or stadium, and hospitality packages. The more unique the experience is, the higher the value. |
| Content | Activation | Other rights |
| Content provided by the football club to implement within the partner's communication and marketing plans. The right to use editorial content such as pictures, video footage, news and statistics. | The right to activate and engage the partner's target audience, leveraging the partnership in the partner's marketing activities. This can be done in different club locations such as the stadium, museum, or training centre. Examples of activation possibilities are on-pitch entertainment, sampling, win-tickets, or digital activations. | The right for the partner organisation to enter the football club's community includes all other partners and related companies. These rights could include things related to the community / CSR projects, the club's mascot, business club events, or keynote presentations. |

# Trends

Whenever I consult football clubs outside the top-five leagues, they often ask for examples of smaller teams. They believe best practice models are built on sporting results without realising that most of the bigger football clubs are built on clear intellectual property and value propositions. Focussing on creating a brand identity and value proposition will enhance rights values and attract brands that share or are interested in sharing the same values.

As an example, we will look at the UEFA Champions League brand. Almost everyone knows its vision: to create the ultimate stage for Europe's Club

Championship. Its mission is to give fans the best club football competition in the world. They hold values such as passion – excellence – inspiration, and authenticity. Their personality can be described as prestigious and exciting. Everyone has these exact feelings when encountering anything related to the UEFA Champions League. Be it the legendary anthem or seeing the iconic fictional stadium made from stars.

The English Premier League did a rebranding in 2016 as there were no clear brand values and too many iterations of the corporate logo. Their rebranding showed ambitious, inspiring, fair, and connectivity values. Ever since their rebranding, the league has grown nationally and internationally.

As times are changing rapidly, sponsorship packages cannot stay behind. New sponsorship categories are being developed as brands want to focus more on fan activation instead of on sports content itself. The digital evolution is an important factor in this. It is also the reason for the growing influence of the second and third screen, which means that those who watch live sports on television also watch simultaneously on their mobile phone and sometimes on a laptop or tablet.

## Brand's view

Why do brands sponsor sports in general and football specifically? One main reason is that sports and football fans are emotionally connected to their sports team or the athletes they support. Building that emotional relationship with customers is very challenging for an ordinary brand. Apart from the emotional connection a brand can achieve with its potential customers through sponsorship, the reach and marketing pool of football clubs are enormous. Football is the most popular sport worldwide and in each country in Europe. Many different media channels create content for fans to consume. Another reason football is so popular for brands to sponsor is that there is content and activities throughout the year. Even during the summer, when there is no competition, there are many stories to tell. Each season starts with new goals, ambition, hope, and excitement to reach those objectives. Finally, the social demographic reach of football fans is wide and yet can be very narrow. The data collection, which almost every football club nowadays has, is of great value for brands.

# Conclusion

The partnership process starts with market research from the football club, analysing all current partner's sectors and the available club assets. Identify the brand's objectives, target audience, and market position. Only approach a brand if you know there is a potential brand fit and the football club can solve multiple issues for the brand. Dare to ask for available budgets after a first introduction meeting. Then take your time to come up with a tailored proposal. Upon acceptance, start planning all campaigns and the different communication channels that are best used. Creativity and innovation are of great importance during the creative development phase. Brands must always be reminded to activate the partnership. This is a two-way relationship, and you are in it together. Even though the activation is the brand's responsibility, their activation results will be part of the partnership evaluation. Therefore, ensure that the club gives proper advice to the sponsor. An evaluation at the end of each campaign or after each season creates a system of improvements and trust. Repeat the cycle by planning the next campaign.

# Key takeaways

- Research what companies are looking for and how you can help to solve their problems.
- Create a partnership strategy that matches your club's identity.
- When drafting the sponsorship pyramid structure, benchmark with other clubs in the same and different leagues but similar in size and assets.
- Always overdeliver on the ROI for brands.
- Data is the new gold to drive value for your sponsors.

# References

AC Milan. (2018a). *Partnership Pillars*. Brussels: AC Milan.
AC Milan. (2018b). *Partnership Process*. Brussels: AC Milan.
*Get Me A Sponsor*. (2016). Retrieved from YouTube: https://www.youtube.com/watch?v=kuzYPv3-MWk&ab_channel=PoonJeevarat

# 16 Ticketing

In the ever-evolving landscape of the global football business, revenue models have shifted and evolved. In the early stages of football globalisation, ticketing was one of the only sources of revenue for football clubs. However, with the introduction of football commercialisation, such as sponsorship and merchandise, ticketing has become less and less of a main revenue generator for football clubs. In the last few decades, with the digitalisation of the industry and rising broadcasting revenues, ticketing revenues have often become less than 10% of football clubs' total revenues. Despite the reduced impact ticketing income has on the total club revenues, many football clubs still have not implemented a beneficial pricing strategy.

For a football club, optimising the relationship between stadium capacity, attendance, and ticketing prices is crucial. Other factors, such as target groups, stadium seat location, and broadcasting camera angles, also play an essential role. However, selling out the stadium by merely lowering prices is misguided and has proven unsuccessful. A better strategy is necessary, and the record and analysis of statistical data on sales, attendance, the economic situation in the region, and the financial situation of various fan groups all play an important role in defining that strategy.

While a higher attendance rate can enhance the atmosphere during games, it only has a small impact on revenues. Football clubs focus on increasing the occupancy rate mainly to build a love brand, as a sold-out or nearly sold-out rate significantly impacts sponsorship negotiations, meetings with the city council, and attracting better players to the club.

Thus, a beneficial pricing strategy is vital for football clubs to optimise revenue streams and build a strong brand. Through proper data analysis and market trends, clubs can find the sweet spot between stadium capacity,

DOI: 10.4324/9781003312680-19

ticket prices, and fan engagement, leading to tremendous success both on and off the field.

# Attendance accelerators

There are several things a football club can control to increase stadium attendance indirectly. A simple way but often forgotten is the comfort of fans in a stadium. Are the seats and toilets clean? Is it easy to find your way around the venue? Can food and beverages be easily gotten, or are there always big queues? What is the quality of the food like? Are there any healthy options? How is the view of the pitch from each seat? Is each seat covered for rain?

Recently a football club asked me to analyse their ticketing strategy as sales have declined for a few years. I walked through the customer journey and analysed each step to find any possible flaws. I was surprised to see that, in May, on the website of the club, there was no information available concerning season tickets for the upcoming season. Furthermore, even at the single ticketing platform, the information available was still from the two years before while there were still COVID restrictions. Keeping the ticketing platform up to date and providing fans with the necessary information is crucial if attendance must increase. Other accelerators are:

- **Sporting results:** Sporting results significantly impact stadium attendance. A big difference is whether a club fights against relegation or competes for the championship. Nevertheless, there are many examples of clubs being nearly sold out even when they are struggling on the pitch or are facing relegation. It cannot be an excuse not to sell out.
- **TV appearance:** The camera angle on television and what someone sees are way more important than you would think. Seeing an empty stadium on television will not excite you to buy a ticket for the next game. Close all sections where the TV cameras are not focussed and only open those sections that are visible on TV if the club is struggling to fill the stadium. Those who watch the game on TV or mobile will see a packed stadium and won't see the empty sections. La Liga implemented this strategy as a regulation for their member clubs; even penalising the clubs if they were not following the regulation. Ever since then, the average stadium attendance in La Liga has grown significantly.

- **Atmosphere:** Something that is not easy to create, but a great atmosphere attracts more fans. Have often meetings with fan groups and create a strategic plan on how the club can support fan groups to create a bigger atmosphere in and around the stadium. Chants, music, smoke, and flares are all part of a football match experience, but everything needs to happen in a safe environment so that everyone can still enjoy attending games. Clear regulations with fan groups will avoid misunderstandings and violence.

- **Stadium Comfort:** Basic things such as clean toilets, comfortable (preferably covered for the rain) seats, trash bins, music installation, and basic hygiene is very standard in any other consumer industry. However, for some reason, many football clubs forget to pay attention to the comfort of their fans.

- **Safety and Security:** Decades ago, the world witnessed the tragedies of hooliganism in football stadiums. Those times had luckily disappeared, but lately, after COVID, multiple issues in various countries have arisen again as fans went back to football games. We have all seen the footage of the relegation match of Saint-Etienne, the chaos after ADO Den Haag missed promotion to the first division, and when the home fans threw flares at the away team fans. Let there be no misunderstanding that fans carry a big responsibility. However, I believe football clubs should do more to protect others and make a safe environment of their stadium for their fans. It starts with treating stewards with respect and giving them all the tools they need to exercise their job. Have a close collaboration with the police department and private security companies. This will not bring the number of issues to zero but talking to the fans might help reducing incidents. Legia Warsaw has a clear policy and has set regulations with their ultra-fans on when, how, and who can use pyro in the stadium. Everything happens in a controlled environment, and the number of issues has been going down yearly.

- **Entertainment:** Tomorrowland has changed the festival industry; it is known worldwide as the most entertaining festival owing to the decoration and multiple acts around the festival. Football clubs will always say that their core business is what happens on the pitch, and they are right. However, is this different for Tomorrowland, and what happens on the stage? Nevertheless, Tomorrowland invested in the infrastructure, decoration, and various acts besides the stage to entertain fans. Football can still learn a lot from other entertainment industries.

- **Club Departments:** Every club department should work closely together to build the best experience for its fans. Marketing, ticketing, hospitality, security, CRM, events, and sports are all involved in a fan's journey and play a role in the entire experience. Having that vision to be an entertaining football club where fans come first will greatly boost attendance.
- **Mobility:** The easier fans can reach the stadium, the better. Nobody likes being stuck in traffic when you want to reach the stadium in time before kick-off. The only issue is that football clubs don't or only in a restricted way control this factor as it has been managed by the government or city council. What football clubs can do is install a safe and secure bike parking next to the stadium and have enough parking available for cars and buses.
- **Match timings:** Something that cannot be controlled either by a football club but has a big impact on fan attendance are the calendar schedule of a match. On a Sunday afternoon? Perfect! *Playing on a Saturday evening or Sunday afternoon is considered the best time for fans to attend football games.* Children and families often will not be able to come to the stadium when a match is played on a Sunday at approximately 9 pm.

Football clubs still see marketing or a season membership campaign as a cost, but the time football sells itself is long past. Football clubs need to attract new fans and a younger generation and invest resources in the renewal of current season card holders. The best strategy for such a marketing plan is to have one main campaign and four sub-campaigns to target specific target groups. The campaign should be focussed on local consumers as they will be the ones to come weekly. International fans can be a focus area for clubs in popular touristic cities, but even then, they should not forget their local fanbase. When launching the dedicated campaign, there should be enough selling points to limit the hassle a fan should go through to buy a season card.

## Revenue accelerator

In the football business, stadium attendance and occupancy rates often go hand in hand. Football clubs such as Manchester United, Bayern Munich, Liverpool, Arsenal, and Borussia Dortmund boast an impressive average stadium occupancy rate of over 90%. While not all stadiums are equally large, the perspective of a full house makes it compelling. The principle of supply and demand applies here – the rarer something is, the more people want it.

A good example was the Champions League final of 2022 in Paris, which was completely sold out. Around 40,000 Liverpool fans flew to Paris to witness the atmosphere in the city or try to buy a ticket for the game. Online, tickets were being sold for over €4,000.-. Similarly, in Belgium, Club Brugge KV has a waiting list for fans eager to buy a season card for the upcoming season, as the stadium is sold out in almost every single game. The less supply there is, the higher the demand, which is evident in the football industry. In conclusion, football clubs with high stadium attendance and occupancy rates tend to benefit from increased ticket demand, which creates a buzz around the club and enhances its brand. The rarity of a sold-out game or a fully occupied stadium only adds to the excitement for fans, and clubs must strategise accordingly to take advantage of this demand.

The cost of individual match tickets is an important revenue accelerator but know that pricing is a serious topic and requires a proper analysis before making any decisions. There is always a risk that fans will not like the increased prices, which will impact the clubs' management image and fan protests. Football clubs often prefer to sell as many season tickets as possible because it is a guaranteed income often received before the start of the season and gives the club a significant boost to its cash flow. The issue from a revenue perspective is that season cards are often sold with a significant discount, and therefore revenues from selling single tickets are much higher. The best proportion rate between season cards and single tickets is often 80/20. However, it is different for each club as it also depends on the economic situation of the region where the club is located. Nevertheless, one of the frustrations of football clubs is fans with a season card only come to the stadium three or four times a season. They occupy their seats for other fans who could have enjoyed a first live match. Various solutions have been offered such as giving seats back for the match if someone cannot come and receiving money if a seat is re-sold. However, despite those efforts, it stayed an issue among many clubs. Brentford FC recently announced a new policy owing to their more than 1,000 unused season ticket holder seats each match. Now every season ticket holder must, when he cannot come to the game, upload his seat that otherwise will not be used on the ticket exchange platform several hours before the match. As of the 2023–2024 season, the club introduces a yellow-card system if the season card holder fails to make his seat available for others when he is not coming to the match. A card cannot be renewed next season if you have four yellow cards before the ticket renewal date for the upcoming 2024–2025 season (Brentford FC, 2023).

Business seats in the stadium are the main driver among ticketing revenue streams. Knowing the demographics well will be crucial to decide how many stadium places you will dedicate to business seats. Fans seated in the business section are often less loud than the die-hard fans behind the goal. As a club director, you still want to have a great atmosphere in the stadium. Try finding the balance between business, family seats, and die-hard stands. The ratio for business seats used to be approximately 10%, but in a newly constructed stadium, that ratio is often much higher and is approximately 20%–25% of the stadium capacity. Of course, the location of the stadium is a big factor in defining the right balance and understanding who the target group is.

Loyalty schemes are often used to build a deeper connection with the fans and to keep them spending money through the different revenue streams. The supporter gains points to their membership profile through purchasing club products such as ticketing, retail, or food & beverages. There are multiple incentives, rewards, and discounts to use at the club or at sponsors of the club. Before a football club introduces loyalty schemes, it should ensure the basics are all in place. This means pricing strategy, communication channels, selling points, CRM system, and the customer journey.

Discounts or giving free tickets away is also a very common thing in many football clubs in the hope of increasing stadium attendance. The thought of a football club 'if they come once, they might come more often afterward' is the wrong approach. Once someone has experienced that they can get something for free, they consider the value of that product to be zero. Why should they pay the following time for the same product they had access to earlier for free? A better idea is to ensure the pricing strategy is well thought off.

## Pricing strategy

Setting the right price for tickets per stadium section is a challenging exercise to do. Start making a benchmark with clubs from the same league and add comparable clubs from abroad to the benchmark. Make a full list of all

Table 16.1 Ticketing Pricing Strategy

| Section | Full price | Price per match | Stand capacity | Occupancy ratio (%) | Note |
|---|---|---|---|---|---|
| Section A | € 205 | € 11 | 8.731 | 100 | The price might be too low |
| Section B | € 350 | € 19 | 4.268 | 12 | Might the price be too high for the section? |
| Section C | € 950 | € 53 | 1.074 | 75 | Good price |
| Section D | € 2.100 | € 117 | 700 | 47 | Price is, OK but maybe focus on sales? |
| Section E | € 600 | € 33 | 2.475 | 5 | Formula/section does not appeal to fans |

the different stand sections, the full price for season card holders, and the price per match. Add a column with the maximum capacity of that stand section and the attendance or occupancy ratio on an entire season base. The analysis should look like this (Table 16.1).

Explain the different pricing for different stand sections to your fans. Analyse the demographics from the groups that all select a similar stadium section. Each section attracts a different type of fan. Make sure that the infrastructure is adapted to the need of each fan group, as it is all about the experience.

# Data is knowledge

Some football clubs implement a ticketing strategy based on assumptions rather than doing the necessary research and discovering the exact motivations of fans behind buying tickets or renewing season cards. Manchester City FC has done that research and discovered that the top three reasons why fans buy season cards are:

1. The fan wants to sit in the same seat every match
2. Want to make sure they can go to every match
3. That no big matches are missed

The slightest reason for fans to buy a season card was 'being attracted by other benefits such as discounts with local suppliers', However, football clubs often use that argumentation as a main selling point in their sales communication. Therefor it is important to invest in research and discover the motivation of fans to come to the stadium, buy season tickets, or choose a specific section in the stadium.

## Key takeaways

- Start increasing attendance before trying to maximise revenues without a sold-out stadium.
- A pricing strategy has a short- and long-term impact on the club and needs to be well considered.
- Data is knowledge. Speak to the fans and understand why the stadium is not sold out weekly.
- The atmosphere is the most undervalued asset of a football club as it attracts fans, and sponsors.

## Reference

Brentford FC. (2023). *Season Ticket Policy Explained*. Retrieved from Brentfordfc. com: https://www.brentfordfc.com/en/news/article/new-brentford-season-ticket-policy-explained

# 17   Hospitality

The uniqueness of hospitality packages is often contingent upon a club's infrastructure and ability to organise various formulas. However, even without an exceptional stadium, there are ample opportunities to craft an unforgettable experience for fans and guests by employing a more creative approach that thinks outside the box. Analysis of football hospitality options across numerous clubs and countries has shown that the number of options available is nearly limitless. However, regardless of the formula used, the ultimate goal is always to provide exceptional entertainment and delicious cuisine.

Football clubs offer various packages and options to prospective VIP guests, but this can also create confusion and errors. While researching hospitality packages offered by English Premier League clubs, it was discovered that one particular club had a three-year-old brochure available for download online. While this is a small mistake, it should not occur, even when numerous communication channels must be updated every time changes are made. Additionally, the brochure for the 2022–2023 season was convoluted and difficult to understand regarding the various packages and options available. To effectively promote their hospitality offerings, clubs should adhere to the fundamental sales principle of 'keeping it simple'.

## Hospitality in general

Football clubs must remember that hospitality extends beyond just catering to VIP guests; it also includes managing the food and beverage experience

DOI: 10.4324/9781003312680-20

for non-VIP fans while meeting their expectations. Fans expect more than just a warm beer and a cold burger. Therefore, following the basic rule of keeping it simple is crucial. There is no need to make it overly complicated. Instead, what do fans truly want?

Fans desire easy access to cold drinks, including beer, water, soft drinks, and hot beverages during colder weather. Additionally, they expect easy access to food close to their seats, with multiple options available. Furthermore, they expect a decent quality of food and at least one healthier option besides burgers and fries. Fast service is also essential to ensure they do not miss any part of the match. An easy payment system is vital for guests who may only visit the venue once. Finally, reasonable prices are crucial for ensuring fans' satisfaction with the overall experience.

These basic elements are essential for each club to provide. A club may consider surveying its fans to identify potential improvement areas if it feels prepared to take things to the next level operationally. Such feedback may include suggestions related to the quality of the food and beverages, different options available, service, and accessibility.

In a stadium, each stand caters to a different type of fan. One stand may be family-oriented, another may cater to premium or VIP guests, and another to the ultras or die-hard fans. However, it is crucial to note that these different fan groups have distinct needs and expectations. A fan survey is an invaluable tool for clubs to collect information to adjust the products and services they offer to their fans. It is essential to consider that most fans have been season cardholders for several years and may have had only one food option available. This leads to potential monotony or a preference for a particular food item, such as a burger becoming a tradition. Therefore, it is crucial to value the fans' opinions and listen to their suggestions.

To enhance the food and beverage experience for fans, football clubs must consider the variation of food, quality of food, and on-seat delivery options. Some clubs have experimented with on-seat delivery, but football stadiums were not built with this in mind, which can pose issues. The space between seats is often insufficient for fans to sit comfortably, let alone allow for someone to pass between seats frequently serving neighbours. While football stadiums could be better designed for food and beverage consumption, even in older stadiums, clubs can try to upgrade the fan experience with some extra care and attention.

# Corporate hospitality

The VIP experience, commonly associated with corporate hospitality, is a crucial aspect of revenue generation for football clubs. Typically, these packages include the best facilities, luxurious interior design, and elegant furniture and are often combined with executive boxes or business seats.

However, it is important to note significant differences between corporate and general in-stadium hospitality, such as dress code, interior design, menu, and beverages. While offering a variation in food choices is essential, providing a range of packages with different prices is equally important. Limiting the number of packages to a maximum of five is advisable to avoid overwhelming potential clients. Nonetheless, if a football club observes that their spectators desire an even more upscale experience, they can create a six-star package, including perks like home pick-up (Table 17.1).

*Table 17.1* Hospitality Packages

| 1. Pub Style Food Bar | 2. Food Market Buffet | 3. Table Service | 4. Table Service | 5. Table Service |
|---|---|---|---|---|
| • Low key | • Low key | • 3 courses | • 4 courses | • 5 courses |
| • Local quality | • Local quality<br>• Better than average brewery | • Better regional quality | • Wine arrangement | • Exclusive wine arrangement |
| | | • Among better restaurants in town | • Different chef per game | • One Michelin star-rated chef for the entire season |
| | | • Dedicated parking area | • Among better restaurants regionally | • Among the better restaurants nationally |
| | | | • Dedicated parking area | • Driver to park your car |
| | | | • Photographer | • Red carpet |
| | | | | • Photographer |

The cuisine offered during corporate hospitality events should be seasonally appropriate and varied for each match. It is important to include options for fish, meat, vegetarian, and alternative dishes for guests with allergies. Online reservation tools and forms can facilitate checking dietary preferences and requirements. Payments for reserved seats and menus should be completed upfront, either in a lump sum or with a cashless payment card distributed at the welcome reception to minimise errors and administration.

In creating a corporate hospitality experience, it is crucial that the facilities are aligned with the intended star system and that prices reflect the quality of the experience offered. It is essential to recognise and charge for the value of the services provided. Mapping out the customer journey for each package can help optimise each experience step to deliver maximum satisfaction.

Football clubs can also learn from other industries, such as equestrian, Formula 1, music festivals, and cultural events, which have set a high standard for hospitality. Tomorrowland dance festival in Belgium is an excellent example of how the environment and a theme can be integrated into the overall experience. It is possible to offer an exceptional experience beyond simply watching a football match.

# Hospitality trends

Customers have increasingly high expectations for exceptional service in the current business climate. Even those opting for a more basic one-star formula anticipate a top-tier experience and demand value for their money. The provision of decent quality food alone no longer suffices; rather, customers desire a memorable encounter that transcends mere culinary excellence. In the past, football clubs emphasised the number of dishes over the experiential and qualitative aspects of their offering. The paradigm has shifted, focussing on immersive dining experiences in unique locations such as the player's tunnel or with an open kitchen featuring a chef's show. Additionally, embracing technology can significantly enhance the speed of service, further elevating the overall customer experience.

# Key takeaways

- Start with doing the basics right.
- This means ensuring that every attendant has easy access to food and beverages and that there are multiple options available.
- Once the basics are all set, start upgrading the quality, order process, payment systems, service, and experiences.
- Ensure the pricing strategy matches the food quality and the story you want to tell.

# 18 Venue management

The stadium, the venue, the home ground, the holy ground of a football club and a city's precious. It is that one building that each city resident knows by heart. It is often a landmark that attracts thousands of tourists to the city and is of great economic value to many businesses. We do not need to explain in detail how important facilities are for football clubs to increase revenues through ticketing, hospitality, sponsorship, non-matchday events, and the merchandise shop. However, it has not always been this way. In the days back, fans just showed up at the stadium, bought a ticket, stood on the hills next to the pitch, and watched their favourite team play with no stands, business seats, merchandise shop, or sponsorship on LED screens. Owing to the tragedies of the Heizel and Hillsborough, a transformation occurred. Football clubs realised that fans cheered and sang for the players when standing or sitting in the stands. However, they opened their wallets when they were inside the skybox or hospitality area.

Owing to the rise of home cinema and better television quality, football clubs had to increase the comfort of the fans at the stadium to compete. Clubs responded by introducing fan zones, fan shops, and fan activations outside the stadium. Since then, the football fan experience has changed a lot, particularly in terms of comfort and cleanliness. However, the entertainment level outside and inside the stadium is at most football clubs still limited. The service towards fans is often slacking behind normal standards or compared to other entertainment industries such as music festivals. Football clubs want to attract fans much earlier to the venue but are not thinking or willing to invest in entertainment areas around the stadium. Note that this

DOI: 10.4324/9781003312680-21

is generally the case, and football clubs are investing to increase stadium atmosphere and matchday experiences.

The demographics of the average football fan are switching rapidly together with their expectations; newly built football stadiums will become increasingly dedicated landmarks and destinations to go to rather than just a football stadium.

# Stadium construction investment

Many new stadiums have been constructed in recent years, and the price tags have been going through the roof. For the construction of a regular stadium, the costs would be, on average, approximately €2.500 per seat capacity. The construction of the new Tottenham Hotspur FC Stadium, with a capacity of 62.850, would have resulted in an average cost of approximately €157.125.000. Nevertheless, the entire project cost approximately €1.110.000.000, and the construction was completed in 2019 (Stadium DB, 2019). That is an average cost of €17.661 per seat. Of course, the stadium has integrated the newest technologies and beautiful architecture, and the pitch can change to an NFL (National Football League) field. However, it is still the question if the club will be able to get a return on investment. When we analyse another recent construction, we see that the investment costs have been much less for a similar capacity: Estadio Metropolitano from Atlético Madrid holds a capacity of 68.450 seats and a price tag of approximately €310 million. Already a big difference from Tottenham's new stadium, but we also need to calculate that Atlético Madrid received €140 million from the city of Madrid for the ground of the old stadium. So, the net investment of Atlético Madrid was approximately €170 million. That is, on average, €2.484 per seat. Another example is the Agia Sophia Stadium from AEK Athens, with a capacity of 32.500 and a total construction cost of around €80.700.000, which results in an average of €2.483 per seat (TFC, 2021). The stadium holds traditional executive boxes, conference rooms, multiple shops, a pool, a wellness area, and a museum. As you can see, the construction of a new stadium or renovation of the current stadium is a big investment. The main question is, will the club make a return on investment in the long run? Furthermore, what is the future of the new football stadiums?

# Stadium as a push or pull factor

A stadium, the venue itself, is important for a football club. It is the theatre where football clubs need to perform and play their games, but each football stadium is also the home of a specific football club. However, does a new stadium always bring success to the club? Before drafting plans for the construction of a new stadium, good market research should be completed. As a modern, new stadium can be a factor that pushes the club to the next level, but it can also be a pull factor that pulls the club down with disastrous results. Multiple factors determine whether a stadium will be a pull or push factor for the club. What factors must we consider to ensure we have a push factor?

- Stadium needs to be consumer-oriented
- Location is crucial
- Create a landmark
- Capacity should match potential market calculation
- A continuous circle is taken into consideration
- Construction costs in relation to economic reality
- Competition (another club in the same neighbourhood)
  - Distance between other clubs for potential derby
  - Distance between clubs can have an impact on potential growth
  - Media coverage in the same region
  - Negotiation power with local government
- Multiple revenue stream possibilities

Some pull factors could be:

- Old infrastructure
- Veblen effect (When the demand is only high if the product is expensive)
- Stadium has no appearance in the city
- Stadium has no other use than one football game every other two weeks
- The athletic track around the pitch
- High safety fences around the pitch
- No comfort for fans
- Financial conditions

Even smaller football stadiums can still be a huge push factor for the football club and the city. A crucial exercise is to calculate the potential in stadium attendance.

On average, 10% of the city population is a maximum attendance potential for a city of 350.000 inhabitants, resulting in an ideal capacity of 35.000 seats. Of course, there are many extra factors to consider, such as the location of the stadium, parking space, public transport access, sporting results, and the popularity of football in the country.

# Seat categories

When constructing a new stadium, there often is a big discussion on what percentage of the total capacity should be allocated to premium hospitality seats and executive boxes. When making a benchmark, we can see that in European football stadiums, the percentage is significantly lower compared to stadiums in America. In Europe, executive boxes and box seat capacity hold approximately 1%–4% of the total stadium capacity. In America, this number increases from 5% to 8%. The differences become even bigger when we take the hospitality suites into account. In Europe, the average is between 4% and 11%, while in America, the average is between 11% and 18%. Nevertheless, a higher hospitality capacity does not always mean more revenues. Iconic football clubs such as Real Madrid or PSG can increase their prices and still sell out every home game owing to its exclusivity.

The demand for hospitality and exclusive experiences is on the rise. Therefore, newly constructed football stadiums should implement a bigger hospitality capacity of 15%–20%.

For Real Madrid (81.000 total capacity), their 245 executive boxes and 2.848 hospitality seats have an estimated revenue potential of €55 million yearly. With a hospitality capacity of 7% over the total capacity, this is already an amazing result. At the AT&T Stadium, the Dallas Cowboys have 25.3% hospitality capacity from the total 80.000 capacity, generating an estimated €156 million yearly (KPMG, 2019). Could this be why Real Madrid is renovating the Santiago Bernabeu? The planned and ongoing renovations are very promising, with an innovative system for pitch retraction. The stadium will be future proof for many years, multiple events can be hosted on non-matchdays, and the overall revenues will increase tremendously.

# Stadium reinvented

Many football clubs are looking to either build an entirely new stadium or renovate their current home ground. However, what makes a stadium future proof and what best practices can football clubs learn from?

The first key factor is the multi-functionality of a football stadium. In the past, most football clubs had an athletic track around the pitch to host athletic events. However, those events were never a source of revenue as the big crowds were not attending these events. Businesses and events that work at football stadiums include conferences, concerts, shopping malls, and schools. The pitch is often the main reason not to host an event, as the grass could be damaged too much. The solution is either a retractable pitch like Schalke04 or Vitesse have or a system where the pitch disappears in the ground, such as Real Madrid will install and OSC Lille already has. The aim is to host events 365 days a year but keep sight of the core business, which is still playing football matches.

One of my biggest frustrations with newly constructed football stadiums is that they are all very similar. There is no room for differentiation, and almost every single seat is the same as the next one, with the same view on the pitch and the same comfort. The only difference between business seats and regular seats is the cushions. This is strange as new football stadiums are no longer becoming iconic landmarks in the city. Additionally, different fan groups come to a football match with different requirements and expectations. For example, the fans in the family stand often bring children with them to watch the match. Unfortunately, when a small child sits on the seat, they will not be able to see the match as the person in front of them is way too tall for them. What often happens is that the child stands up on the seat, resulting in the person behind them not being able to see the match anymore and must stand up as well. A simple solution could be to adjust the seats in the family section in height and fix these seats for all-season cardholders or to give security the ability to adjust the height when a problem occurs.

Seats behind the goal are often reserved for the most passionate fans, those that want to sing, waive with flags, and jump around. Owing to safety issues in the past, standing stands were not allowed for a long time. However, since the introduction of safe standing, this can be organised very safely. These fans do not want a fancy bar or a nice corridor. They want to have a stand that breaths the club's history through graffiti on the walls and to post stickers where they want. Make those safe standing platforms wide enough so people can dance, implement within a new construction a place for a DJ or other artist, so the club does not lose any seats as they need to build a stage to have some fan entertainment before or after the match.

When constructing a new stadium, a solution must be found for the use of pyro. Most of us agree that pyro can be dangerous, but it creates an atmosphere. Instead of fighting against the use of pyro, why not create a safe zone where pyro can be used and where extra safety measures are taken to limit the risk of injuring others? The same accounts for a tifo in the stadium. Legia Warsaw has a safe system where certain fans can use the roof to unroll a tifo over a stand. It is a much safer use as no one can be trapped under it.

For away fans, the stand is often in terrible condition. There is little respect in welcoming fans from other teams with dirty toilets, very limited food and beverage options, and sometimes even a plastic wall as a 'shield' between them and the pitch. Think about the away section at the old Camp Nou from FC Barcelona or at Sint-Truiden VV. Having in mind the saying 'when you treat someone as a beast, he or she will become a beast', it might be a better idea to welcome away fans with respect and kindness. Have a space in the stand with all the necessary elements for a fan shop and rent it to the club playing at the stadium. Make all staff in the away stand to wear a jersey from the away team and work with digital screens and led lights so the colours can be adjusted, and the logo of the away team is very visible on the stand. Violence will decrease, and revenues from the away stand will increase.

Finally, the VIP experience is in almost every stadium the same. It looks like the interior architect is travelling from one stadium to another and designing the same concept repeatedly. Why are football clubs less creative, considering the three important factors for VIP revenue streams: experience, exclusivity, and quality? Unfortunately, in the last decade, no major innovation for a VIP experience at football stadiums has been made. The only change worth mentioning is the tunnel club introduced by Manchester City FC. There is room for improvement, and something unique can be constructed where the experience, exclusivity, and quality come together. Imagine an impressive entrance such as the one from Sagrada Familia in Barcelona, walking on a red carpet where photographers take pictures from VIP fans and their guests. The members' card is ready at the reception and requires the member's mobile phone to be deposited in a personal safe as no pictures are allowed to be taken to keep the mystery of the experience. Dinner begins in the dining room or have tapas on a balcony. Those who prefer to watch a concert, an artist or sort of performance can go to the theatre, and those who want to watch football match can go to the stands. See it as a double event in the same venue with joint hospitality areas.

# Key facility factors

Based on multiple surveys, football fans have indicated what they believe are the key factors that make a facility excellent. It is no surprise that the match and stadium atmosphere are ranked as number one. Therefore, we advise listening more carefully to the fans and adjusting new stadium plans to their needs to create an amazing atmosphere. Other key factors are the cleanliness of the stadium, hospitality (prices, access, range, quality), welcoming and kindness of the staff, mobile signal, facilities for children, and sightlines in the stadium.

# Key takeaways

- Football clubs rely heavily on their home stadiums as a major revenue source.
- The attractiveness of the stadium is key to drawing in fans, sponsors, players, and other stakeholders.
- Many football stadiums are owned by municipalities, often resulting in missed revenue opportunities for clubs.
- Non-matchday events offer a way for clubs to build deeper connections with fans and generate additional revenue.
- Modern stadiums tend to lack creativity and personalised solutions for different fan groups.
- Clubs can differentiate themselves by prioritising innovative stadium designs tailored to their unique contexts and fan bases.
- Clubs can increase fan engagement, enhance revenue streams, and strengthen their position in the industry by creating a customised stadium experience.

# References

KPMG. (2019). *KPMG Stadium Benchmark*. KPMG.

Stadium DB. (2019). *Tottenham Hotspur Stadium*. Retrieved from stadiumdb.com: http://stadiumdb.com/stadiums/eng/tottenham_hotspur_stadium

TFC. (2021). Retrieved from TFC Stadiums: https://tfcstadiums.com/future-agia-sophia-stadium/

# 19 Merchandise

The fundamental aspect of a football club centres around the players and their on-pitch activities. The players represent the club's main attraction and the focus of nearly all operations within the football organisation. The sale of tickets, sponsorship, and merchandise, which has become an integral part of the football business, is primarily driven by the commercialisation of the game and the need to pay players higher salaries. Nevertheless, the primary objective of football clubs was never to distribute tickets or sell sponsorship assets or merchandise. With the growth of the game and the increasing salaries of players, clubs had to explore and develop new revenue streams. This chapter will discuss merchandise development within the football industry, including its supply chain, logistics, distribution, and innovative technology.

Merchandise sales target club fans, including families, business club members, ultras, and children. However, the challenge of meeting the diverse desires of these fan groups, including different clothing styles and sizes, combined with the complexities of supply chain management, distribution channels, and delivery, makes selling merchandise a complicated matter. This is one of the reasons why many football clubs prefer to work with a third party to manage their merchandise, even though this may result in a loss of potential revenue. Some football clubs focus solely on their match-going fans or the clubs' supporters, thereby missing out on the bigger picture.

Considering the worldwide popularity of football clubs in general, and the size of the retail industry, it is surprising that merchandise income is only a small part of a club's total revenue.

DOI: 10.4324/9781003312680-22

# Target group

As we mentioned above, the target group for football clubs to sell their merchandise to is often focused on the fans of the club or even only on those that attend matches. However, only some fans are happy with the commercialisation of their beloved football club and the rising costs of ticketing, food & beverages, and merchandise. Take, for example, football jerseys. Top football clubs such as Real Madrid or PSG have partnerships with the biggest sports brands such as adidas or Nike and have three newly designed shirts each year; a home, away, and third jersey. In the case of Real Madrid, they even developed a fourth unique FIFA jersey for the popular console game FIFA (now EA Sports FC). Since Napoli closed a collaboration with Emporio Armani in 2021, they present ten different jerseys in one season, with a price tag of €125 per jersey. It is one of the reasons why football fans feel neglected and left out by the over-commercialisation of their beloved team.

Is co-branding a solution to have a bigger reach and develop a consumer base outside of the fan group of a football club? One of the latest examples of co-branding is the partner between PSG and the Jordan Brand. Nike saw a great opportunity to partnering with PSG to reach new audiences and geographical areas. The same applied to PSG, where they saw an opportunity to enter North America. In a few years, the United States of America became PSG's second-biggest market, with a share of 11%. The club's strategy was to transform PSG into a global lifestyle brand beyond football fans. Of course, being in Paris, the fashion capital, and the demographical diversity of the city, in combination with the geographical diversity of the players, were the perfect ingredients for this collaboration.

The downside of quick growth or sudden sporting success is that football clubs are often not prepared for the fans' demands. When Leicester City FC became the English Premier League champions in 2016, the club ran out of replica shirts to sell as the club was unprepared for the increased sales. Nobody at the club thought it would be possible to win the Premier League, the club did not increase their stock at the beginning of the season, and thus they sold out in record times. In the next season, the club sold ten times as many shirts in 24 hours as it did in the first month of the previous season. Something similar happened at Ajax FC in 2021. The club launched its new third kit inspired by the Bob Marley song Three little birds and sold out in no time. Records were broken, and the shirt is listed as the most popular shirt in the club's history. Not only fans of Ajax FC bought the third kit, but many international football fans also want to have the jersey as a collector's item because of what it stands for. These examples show that football fans love an underdog story such as Leicester City FC and that football clubs can influence sales through brand management and storytelling. Unfortunately, many clubs still lack creativity or do not negotiate their technical partnership well and therefore have no say in the design.

# Distribution channels

In the ever-evolving world of retail, even football clubs are not immune to the challenges of meeting dynamic demand. Several football clubs, including Leicester City FC and Ajax FC, have encountered issues with sudden increases in demand from fans worldwide who wish to purchase their merchandise online. However, owing to a lack of global delivery infrastructure, many fans face difficulties and additional costs in receiving their orders. The supply chain channels involved in manufacturing, assembling, transporting, selling, and delivering products are complex. They involve various factors such as information, product designs, finance, price strategies, risks, and more. Distribution channels can be particularly challenging owing to the rapidly evolving technology, complex data transactions between companies due to GDPR, difficulty predicting supply and demand, and the increasingly international focus of clubs whose operations remain primarily national.

Despite these challenges, it is surprising that many football clubs are still primarily focused on their stadium shops, even if the stadium is not located in an area with high traffic or nearby shops. The expectation that fans will drive to the stadium during the week between 9 am and 5 pm to purchase merchandise is unrealistic. It is essential to consider alternative options. Opening a shop in the city centre, preferably in the main shopping street, may be a better choice, as it provides visibility for the club and allows for more outstanding communication of other messages, such as upcoming home matches or sponsorship opportunities. While some clubs argue that such shops are not profitable, making a physical shop profitable with a clear brand and merchandise strategy is possible.

Leading football clubs like PSG and Real Madrid have multiple shops in their home city and abroad, in crowded places such as airports or shopping malls. These shops allow international fans to experience the brand and provide an opportunity to own a piece of the club. Rather than solely focusing on increasing turnover, these clubs see merchandising as a way to bring their brand to the streets as a marketing product, which ultimately boosts turnover.

Unfortunately, many clubs still need a decent web shop, and their websites are often not translated into the main languages their international fans speak. Such clubs may experience significant potential revenue losses, particularly when an international hype occurs organically, and the necessary delivery and payment systems still need to be set up to meet the demand. Failing to prepare such systems can harm a club's reputation and affect its revenue in the long term.

# Licensing

Despite their lack of recent sporting success, Manchester United's continued dominance at the top of Deloitte's Football Money League can be attributed in part to their successful licensing agreements across the globe. The club's enduring brand value, supported by a large and devoted fan base, ensures that many individuals continue to purchase Manchester United merchandise, contributing substantially to the club's revenues. It is important to understand the concept of licensing in this context.

When a company seeks to enter a specific region and believes that the desired business objectives can be achieved through the fan base of a football club, a licensing agreement can be reached between the retailer and the club. This agreement typically involves using the club's badge, name, colours, images, and other relevant elements of the retailer. The retailer pays the football club a fee, which may be a fixed upfront payment, a percentage of the product's sales, or a combination of both. With the licence, the retailer can market the product in the agreed-upon region, customised with the club's badge, colours, or other relevant elements. One of the key advantages of licensing is that it involves no production costs or inventory risks for the club. However, the downside is that the club only receives a percentage of the revenues, while most of the profit goes to the retailer.

The decision to license or merchandise depends on various factors, such as the club's business model, available resources, expertise, and risk assessments for capital expenditure investments and inventory management. The club should thoroughly analyse to determine whether a product is consistent with its objectives, brand values, target audience, distribution channels, and existing sponsorship structure.

# Logistics

In the context of a football club, logistics refers to the management of the supply chain involved in bringing merchandise and equipment to the club and distributing it to customers and fans worldwide. The logistics process begins with arranging for storage of all the club's stock, including player kits, merchandise, and other equipment. This often involves managing warehouses that can accommodate the club's ever-changing demands, as fan interest and player transfers can create unexpected surges in demand. The European Club Association explains the challenges of logistics as follows.

Once the stock is stored away, keeping an inventory of the entire stock is crucial. In football, where the environment changes rapidly due to player transfers and the expectation of fans that clubs should release new kits each year, managing inventory is essential to avoid either running out of stock for popular products or being left with excess stock at the end of the season or from a particular football player who has already left the club after a transfer (European Club Association, 2018).

Packaging is also an important consideration for football clubs in the logistics process. It is important for protecting and ensuring the safety of merchandise during transportation and carries important information for customers and operational processes. Football clubs can leverage packaging as an opportunity to communicate with their fans by ensuring their packaging is branded and shares a message with customers.

Transportation is another crucial aspect of logistics for football clubs, as customers worldwide expect quick delivery times. Establishing a partnership with an experienced logistics partner who can deliver packages internationally can help ensure timely and efficient delivery.

Finally, effective communication between different departments within the football club is essential to increase work efficiency and reduce errors. The digitalisation of logistics processes can help to facilitate this communication and streamline the overall logistics process.

# Products

Regarding the merchandise offered by football clubs, it is important to carefully consider the products that will resonate with fans and drive sales.

Before making any decisions, conducting thorough market research is essential to understand better the demographics of the core fans and those who live further away and may be more likely to shop online. This research will help guide the selection of products and inform the development of a communication plan to sell each product, including pricing strategies and margins effectively.

One club that has successfully developed its product range is Hungary's Ferencvaros Torna Club. In addition to a formal clothing line and casual leisure products, they have also created a special edition merchandise line for the ultra-fans of the club, referred to as 'Fradi'. Furthermore, Ferencvaros has licensed manufacturers to produce whisky, protein bars, and crackers.

Designing merchandise involves carefully considering various factors, including quality, style, and branding. Pricing strategies must be developed to maximise profitability while remaining competitive with other clubs. Additionally, interior shop design must be considered to create a welcoming environment that reflects the club's brand and enhances the overall fan experience (Table 19.1).

*Table 19.1* Football Merchandise Products

| Match wear | Team Kit | Footwear | |
| | Balls | Protection | |
| Training gear | Balls | Footwear | Training Accessories |
| | Training Kit | Protection | Coaching Accessories |
| Clothing | Leisure | Casual | Headwear |
| | Formal | Ultra-designs | Underwear |
| Living | Watches | House accessories | Other Sports |
| | Leather goods | Outdoor | Boardgames |
| Work/school | Backpack | Wrapping paper | |
| | Pen & notebook | Diary | |
| Health | Grooming | Food & Beverages | |
| | Nutrition | | |
| Travel | Bags | Towels | |
| | Trolley | Toilet facilities | |
| Electronics | Headphones | Charger | Gaming |
| | Mobile cover | Toaster | |

# Merchandise process

In the world of professional football business, designing and producing merchandise products is a crucial part of generating revenue and increasing fan engagement. The first and foremost rule of designing merchandise products is to know the target market. Fan profiles can be analysed through CRM systems, which provide insight into sex, age, average income, and location. When designing merchandise, it is important to consider the club's identity and brand guidelines. Elements such as the club crest, fonts, pantone colours, secondary branding assets, club nicknames, and formation year should all be considered. Emotive associations such as the stadium as a landmark, fan chants and anthems, or players, legends, and popular managers can also be considered.

Once the strategies for designs and products have been prepared, the next step is to find the right suppliers that provide the best advantages to the club. It is not necessary to have one supplier for all merchandise products. Sports merchandise trade shows are a great way to meet suppliers and feel their products before ordering them. The 'workbook' is one of the most important documents within retailing, as it contains all the necessary details about the product, including crest or branding possibilities, such as double twill with zig-zag stitches or 3D embroidery.

Ordering merchandise can be challenging, as it requires keeping track of previous sales to estimate future sales accurately. The popularity of a football club often depends on the sporting performances or media attention it generates. For example, Chelsea FC sells approximately 1.5 million jerseys yearly, while clubs like Real Madrid and Manchester United sell over 3 million jerseys yearly. Smaller teams typically have lower sales numbers that fluctuate more depending on the design and customer opinion. The first step in the ordering process is identifying the requirements for each product in every category. The second step is to research suppliers, including whether other sports teams are selling the same item, delivery possibilities, and more. Thirdly, it is time to go into more detail with potential suppliers, discussing minimum order quantity, cost price per unit, package options, development and production times, and any changes that can be made to the product. After thorough research and a sample product check, a preferred supplier is selected. The supplier will then start working on product development and propose computer-aided designs to agree on the final product specifications. After the purchase order has been signed, the manufacturing process begins. The club often receives samples for approval, and the final stage of the sampling and development process is known as the 'Gold Seal' approval.

# Pricing strategy

In football, clubs must set an annual KPI margin target to achieve their revenue goals. However, this target can be influenced by several factors, including increased branded wholesale prices, sourcing of own-label products, logistic services costs, brand exposure rebate contributions, and product pricing.

While the overall annual margin target for most football clubs is approximately 40%, this does not mean that every product yields a 40% margin. For example, the margin for training kits is typically lower at around 25%–30%, whereas margins for popular items such as scarves, headwear, socks, and replica jerseys can reach as high as 55%–75%. The net cost price is multiplied by 2.5. For instance, if a product costs €10 plus VAT, the recommended retail price would be €25 to determine the recommended retail price (RRP).

Of course, a football club's level of play can impact pricing. For example, in the Premier League, the RRP is typically three and a half times higher compared to the national league, where the RRP is only one and a half times higher. Other pricing factors include location, demographics, affluence, and fan base.

The life cycle of products in football merchandise typically ranges from nine to twelve, or at most eighteen, months. Implementing a sales or discount strategy is necessary to avoid having a large stock of unsold merchandise. Ideally, a sales strategy is preferred, and most football clubs use three phases of sales: the normal sale, which typically involves a 10%–20% discount; phase two, which sees a 30%–40% discount; and phase three, where a discount of over 50% is offered. This gradual reduction in selling price stimulates sales for a particular product, and the discount level can be increased as required to drive sales volume in line with demand. It is important to remember that clubs often still profit even when offering discounts. When new product lines are introduced and the old stock remains, clubs will reduce the margin to 5% to drive rapid sales and clear out the remaining stock of a particular product.

# Fan shop design

The physical fan shop plays a crucial role in driving merchandise sales in football. While larger clubs like Real Madrid, Manchester City FC, and FC Barcelona boast enormous fan shops with many products, smaller clubs outside of major cities are pressured to be innovative and attract fans to their physical stores, especially in the wake of rising online sales.

So, what makes an excellent fan shop? Aside from the importance of customer service, product availability, and efficient speed of service, a successful fan shop engages with its customers, offers a unique experience, and has a clear flow direction. Collaboration with kit partners such as adidas, Nike, or Puma can provide a store improvement budget for a cosmetic makeover of the fan shop. For instance, Arsenal FC has partnered with adidas to create an augmented reality skills zone in their fan shop, while other clubs focus on creating large meeting spaces for players to give speeches or answer Q&As or integrate eSports to create a more digitalised experience.

To illustrate this point further, look at Stoke City FC's merchandise sales strategy. The club has two major stores, one at the stadium and another in the city centre, complemented by a robust online webshop. Despite its smaller size and lower profile, Stoke City FC sells approximately 40,000 replica home and away jerseys yearly, a remarkable achievement highlighting the importance of effective merchandise sales strategies.

Stoke City FC keeps its organisational structure lean and efficient, with two store managers overseeing a store, four warehouse staff, a retail buyer, and a head of retail. Limited staff in a clear organisational structure is a cost-efficient strategy that increases the profit margin. One of the major risks for football clubs is stock leftovers at the end of the season. Therefore, major promotions such as 24 h flash sales or three for two offers are critical to driving sales during holidays. Discounting the stock from January to May is also important to prevent stockpiling and potential losses for the upcoming season. A clear pricing strategy for the entire season is essential in reducing the stock without incurring losses.

In summary, a successful fan shop offers quality products and excellent service and offers customers a unique and engaging experience. Effective organisational structures, merchandise sales strategies, and pricing policies are all essential components of a successful fan shop that can help smaller clubs compete with their larger counterparts in the ever-evolving world of the football business.

# Key takeaways

- As CRM is important in every club department, data will greatly influence which retail strategy to follow and define the target group.
- Ensure that the basics work and that customers can order and purchase merchandise smoothly.
- Logistics and stock management are challenging when running a merchandise store is not the core activity of a football club. Work with specialists that have experience.
- Dare to offer unique products/designs to customers, give them a platform to think along, and ask their opinion.
- The pricing strategy needs to be on point and adjusted to the level the club is playing at.
- Physical stores still hold value, and if you are located in a bigger city, a store in the stadium and one in the city centre would be perfect.

# Reference

European Club Association. (2018). *Club Management Guide*. ECA.

# Business development

## 20

Simon Van Kerckhoven and
Martijn Ernest

Growth strategies are essential for increasing total revenues and club valuation in the football club context. While many factors are unique to the football industry, it is still possible for clubs to use the four main principles of business growth strategies. In this regard, we outline the following growth strategies: market penetration, product development, market development, and diversification.

- *Market Penetration* involves increasing sales of existing products or services in existing markets to increase market share. Football clubs can increase revenue by promoting and selling more season cards, single tickets, merchandise, and hospitality packages. However, since reducing prices is only sometimes a viable option, football clubs can adopt an increased promotion or temporary discount approach such as early bird tickets or taking a friend. Nonetheless, a sound pricing and marketing strategy can significantly impact market penetration.
- *Product Development* aims to launch new products or services in existing markets. This approach may increase the turnover of current customers. Football clubs can develop new products through investment in research and development, acquisition of rights to produce someone else's product, buying in the product and 'branding' it, or joint development with ownership of another company that needs access to the firm's distribution channels or brands. An example of product development in football clubs is the implementation of licensing in merchandise strategies. With a decline in season card holders, fan attendance, and broadcasting rights, football clubs have started to explore new products

DOI: 10.4324/9781003312680-23

such as eSports, women's football, exclusive content creation on social media, and NFTs and fan tokens.

- *Market Development* entails increasing existing product or service sales in previously unexplored markets. For football clubs, this often involves internationalisation, taking the brand to an international level. Football clubs can achieve this by playing pre-season games abroad, sponsoring activation events abroad, and opening offices or stores in foreign countries. A multi-club ownership strategy can also be used to explore new fanbases and markets to be linked with the club or at least to have access to data generated by other clubs in different markets.

- *Diversification* involves launching new products or services in previously unexplored markets, the riskiest growth strategy. However, the biggest growth potential for football clubs can be achieved by developing a diversification strategy. There are four different types of diversification: horizontal, vertical, concentric, and conglomerate.

a. **Horizontal Diversification**

This involves purchasing or developing new products by the football club, to sell them to the existing fanbase. These new products are often technologically or commercially unrelated to current products but may appeal to current fans. Fan tokens and football club electric bikes are good examples of horizontal diversification.

b. **Vertical Diversification**

This involves the football club entering the sector of its suppliers or fans. For instance, the football club acquires a catering company to manage all food & beverages at the stadium, sets up a marketing company that handles all their social media accounts or develops a brewery to produce a unique football club beer.

c. **Concentric Diversification**

This strategy involves the development of a new line of products or services with technical or commercial similarities to an existing range of products. An example of this can be manufacturing football balls or football jerseys.

d. **Conglomerate Diversification**

This approach involves moving into new products or services with no technological or commercial relation with current products, equipment, or distribution channels but may appeal to new groups of customers.

An example could be a football club developing its car or investing in furniture or solar panels.

Within the world of football, we have seen many clubs using market penetration and product development as growth strategies. Bigger football clubs such as AC Milan, Manchester United FC, Bayern Munich, and Real Madrid have also developed a market development strategy. Nevertheless, those clubs benefitted greatly owing to their sporting results in domestic and UEFA competitions. We must admit that Ajax FC's growth strategies may be one of the best examples within football, but also, some less famous teams are growing owing to the implementation of a clear strategy. Many football clubs can still develop themselves through market development and a diversification growth strategy. Let us analyse those two strategies further.

# Market development

Globalisation and internationalisation have been buzzwords to describe the integration of markets and the benefits (or dis-benefits) of economic relationships. The integration of football into the global economy represents a double challenge for all those involved with the sport and for the future of the sport itself. Conversely, all these developments constitute new exciting and profitable opportunities. In contrast, the identities and traditions that embody football are being questioned and stressed (Beek, 2019).

Owing to the growing global interest in football via the creation of global fan communities and the saturation of the domestic football market, football clubs are looking to transcend the traditional structure of the football business by relying on their internationalisation strategy as an important growth driver. Finding new revenue streams and monetising international brand recognition is the ultimate goal (European Club Association, 2015). As opportunities for football clubs are numerous, we will first delve deeper into the requirements to monetise international expansion. We focus on some strategic focus areas and market entry strategies before finishing with best practices from all over Europe. We emphasise that this potential revenue optimisation can only be successful when it fits the club's overall strategy and when the football club is ready in each department.

- **Requirements:** For a football club to expand internationally success-fully, it is crucial first to evaluate its position in the domestic market. It may not be feasible or appropriate for all clubs to pursue global expansion. Therefore, the football entity should assess whether it has already reached its commercial potential at the national level. The club may be better off diversifying its operational services rather than expanding to far-flung markets if there is still room for growth. In contrast, if the club has exhausted its potential in the domestic market, it is time to develop a strategy that aligns with its brand and identity.

  The club should create a process that encourages a free flow of ideas, goods, services, capital, and people, integrating societies and economies to attract an international audience. It is beneficial for the club to have a strong league open to innovation and expansion, focussing on selling international broadcasting rights to establish overseas connections. The club should also have sufficient financial resources to support the investment required for international expansion. The club must have a well-defined brand identity, vision, and values that are attractive to an international audience. Having international club ambassadors, such as former players and players from growing markets, and participation in international club competitions, such as the UEFA Champions League, Europa League, or the Conference League, can also help attract an international audience.

- **Strategic Focus Areas:** As previously mentioned, certain pre-requisites must be met for a football club to establish itself as an international brand. However, it is important to note that a club can be situated in a different area than Europe's major cities or even incorporate famous landmarks, such as the Eiffel Tower, in its branding to expand its reach into new markets. Clubs should rather focus on the products and services they can offer to a global audience to make their brand visible world-wide. Venezia FC is doing an amazing job by staying consistent and loyal to the brand.

  While some football clubs may get into the international market with the sole intention of generating quick profits, it is worth noting that these short-term gains are often elusive and difficult to achieve. Rather, a commitment to long-term success is often more beneficial. Many of the most successful European football clubs have established youth academies, corporate social responsibility programs, pre-season training camps and friendlies, partnerships, and even stores in foreign markets.

Before a football club can successfully expand its business activities internationally, it must determine how to make its various products, such as the first team, U21 team, youth academy, women's team, eSports, and community trust, attractive to a non-domestic market. This process begins with developing a marketing and communication plan based on the club's brand identity for each core asset. This requires identifying the unique selling points of each asset and determining how best to communicate these to an international audience.

Once the club has determined how to attract potential consumers, it must focus on creating awareness of its products. Two key factors in this phase are media exposure and commercial interest. The club's activities will gradually transition from being merely visible to becoming hot and eventually loved by consumers by spreading the word that the club's products are available in a new market via media channels and implementing targeted marketing strategies.

Finally, the club must capitalise on its investment by selling its products. This return on investment can be achieved through various means, such as merchandising, ticket sales, or corporate partnerships. Ultimately, the success of a football club's international expansion efforts will depend on its ability to position itself effectively in new markets and leverage its unique assets to create lasting relationships with global consumers (Table 20.1).

- **Market Entry Strategies:** After being aware of the club's assets and all possible activities which can be used to engage with consumers in non-domestic markets, the three most prevailing models football clubs are using to increase their engagement with international markets are: (Pueckler, 2015)

1. The Uppsala Model can be described as a market entry approach, which requires a company to enter a new, international market in four stages: sporadic exports, use of agents, use of sales partnerships, and use of owned subsidiaries. In the first stage, football clubs usually interact with the targeted market very irregularly. The objective is to study the response of consumers in the target market. Once the response from the first stage turns out to be positive, the second stage is to seek sales agents with a physical presence in the target market. However, these agents are expected to be from local entities with a good understanding of the dynamics of the international market. The

Table 20.1 Using Assets to Create Extra Revenue Streams

| Sport related activities | Commercial matchday sales | Commercial non-machday sales | Public relations |
|---|---|---|---|
| • International friendlies & tournaments<br>• Pre-season tours<br>• Seasonal training camps<br>• Academies<br>• Consultancy on sporting and technical development to other football industry stakeholders<br>• Consultancy on youth development to other football industry stakeholders | • Viewing parties<br>• Ticket sales | • Paid content via OTT platform streaming<br>• Broadcasting rights<br>• Merchandise via fan shop<br>• Merchandise via an e-commerce platform<br>• Cultural events<br>• Product licensing<br>• Partnerships and sponsoring<br>• Paid membership scheme<br>• Museum visits<br>• Consultancy on commercial developments to other football industry stakeholders<br>• NFTs<br>• Fan Tokens | • Corporate Social Responsibility<br>• Institutional and governmental collaborations<br>• Contributions to press channels (online and offline)<br>• Acquisition of other football clubs |

next stage calls for a close partnership with a local company if the use of agents is successful.

2. There is a bigger presence in the foreign market at this stage, but the feasibility study continues. The final stage is used as a permanent entry to disclose relevant products in the target country. Mind that this strategy requires a football club to increase its international model gradually, and results will only be visible after a very long time.

3. The Transaction Cost Approach Model is preferable for new market entrants. The football club seeks to identify a local club or company that it finds viable and competitive for that market and directly invests in or creates a partnership with this local football club by using this model.

4. This strategy is considered cost-effective because it is a form of international merger that does not require a physical start-up in the international market. This started with football clubs setting up collaborations, such as Atlético de Kolkata in India, partnering with Atlético de Madrid, and later evolving to the multi-club ownership model which has become a dream for many investors.

5. The Industrial Network Approach Model requires the football club seeking to go international to identify several local companies that share the same philosophy and values and then follow the same procedure as the transaction cost strategy. However, the difference is that the company seeks internationalisation partners with the local entity rather than investing in it. This means that the merger issue does not apply in the case of industrial network strategy since there is no financial commitment to the local company. Rather than a financial commitment, the football club ensures that the local entity is engaged in a service or product sector with the prospect of introducing a new service or product in the market.

- **Does it really fit the club's overall strategy?:** As stated before, not all clubs can uphold a strategy towards internationalisation. It needs to fit the overall brand and geographical/economic status quo. However, clubs cannot set up this strategy should not see this as a failure or mismanagement. There is nothing wrong with not being able to develop internationally as long as they keep catching up with the development of the modern football business through improvements in management, infrastructure, club branding, media rights, marketing, commercialisation, and the general monetisation of domestic football products. As we discussed earlier, a football club can be at a local, regional, domestic, or international level. A good strategy is going step by step forward towards the next level in a consistent way.
- **Best practices from all over Europe:** Let us take a closer look at some best practices in Europe. After analysing the European football landscape, these clubs can be seen as frontrunners and innovators in growing their business internationally. For each club, an answer is given to these questions:

  - What is their strategy? – general product and activation
  - Which main activities do they have? – one best practice per club
  - What is the main result? – achievement

Red Bull Salzburg

- **Strategy:** First Team – Content via OTT Platform
- **Main Activity:** Documentary on Red Bull TV

- **Main Result:** The Red Bull brand is everywhere, and Red Bull's brand is what drives the football club. Red Bull has headquarters in Austria; no wonder they sponsor a football club. They have taken it to the next level: Red Bull Racing, AlphaTauri, New York Red Bulls, FC Red Bull Salzburg, RB Leipzig, Red Bull Bragantino, EHC Red Bull München, and EC Red Bull Salzburg. One-way Red Bull Salzburg profits from this absolute brand alignment are by producing a new documentary, JederMann – This is Salzburg. Not only does this provide the club with content they can use on their own platforms, but it also gives lots of potential consumers the ability to get in touch with them via Red Bull's OTT platform.

Leicester City FC

- **Strategy:** First Team – Post-Season Tour
- **Main Activity:** Thailand trip
- **Main Result:** After winning the Premier League in 2016, plans were stepped up for the first team's tour to Thailand, the home of the club's owners, King Power. While no game or open training session was planned, a meet and greet with the local LCFC fan clubs and business meetings were on the schedule. Four years later, the club has a solid fan base in Asia and numerous partners involved f.e. Bia Saigon, Chang & Yabo. The sporting results had a huge impact on the internationalisation of Leicester City FC, but this only sped up the process of a great strategic plan in a market where few competitors are active.

Olympique Lyonnais

- **Strategy:** eSports – Non-Matchday Events
- **Main Activity:** Global eSports strategy
- **Main Result:** Olympique Lyonnais has entered the world of eSports by relying on the main components of its expertise, football, and competition. Creating this eSports team fits into the club's project to expand its activities throughout different areas and get closer to the Olympique Lyonnais community by sharing online experiences worldwide. LDLC OL will compete in major eSports tournaments, pushing the Olympique Lyon brand to new consumers who are not to be reached via the traditional communication tools of a football club. In addition to acquiring

an eSports team, the club also invests in the construction of an eSports arena to organise tournaments and host various events.

## Vfl Wolfsburg

- **Strategy:** Sustainability – Sports Science – Fan Experiences
- **Main Activity:** Entering blockchain, NFTs, and the metaverse
- **Main Result**: Nobody knows the future of NFTs and the metaverse. However, as it is a new emerging market for everyone, the club is fully aware that this market will have a crash and is preparing for that. The club sees NFTs as collectibles, gamification, and utility. Collectibles are what humans have always done and will continue to love to do, only now in a digital way. Gamification as games will always be there, and anything around fantasy gaming will survive such a potential crash. The utility is the most important part of the NFT strategy, as this brings value to the NFT. VfL Wolfsburg partnered up with The Football Company, an NFT start-up, to create a fantasy game where the NFTs of the club have a utility within the game. The next step is to bring that digital NFT utility into the real world. For example, by buying a specific NFT, you could have a personal interview and meeting with one of the players. This strategy made the club stronger in markets such as China and the United States.

## FC St Pauli

- **Strategy:** Overall Club – Merchandising (E-Commerce)
- **Main Activity:** Rock 'N Roll Football Campaign
- **Main Result:** Technically speaking, FC St. Pauli is a football club from Hamburg, Germany. The Truth is, it is way more than that. It is a lifestyle, an attitude. With their left-wing, punk rock fan base, St. Pauli stands against fascism, racism, sexism, and homophobia. It is a movement that is brought forward with like-minded people. At the same time, it is the most Rock'n'Roll sports club in the world – or have you ever seen another sports team walk on the field to AC/DC's Hells Bells? Coinciding with their brand-new American web shop – their clothing line embraces the rebellious spirit of the eponymous red-light district in Hamburg – St. Pauli is bringing its unique spirit across the pond, endorsing with several punk rock bands. All this is centralised on a designated website. Having a consistent and unique brand identity pays off.

FC Basel

- **Strategy:** Football Club Acquisition
- **Main Activity:** Minority stake in Chennai City FC
- **Main Result:** In 2019, FC Basel became the first European club to make a major investment (26%) in Indian football, taking a substantial stake in the southeast Indian team Chennai City FC. The 20 million EURO investment went directly to setting up a training centre. Furthermore, the partnership includes creating a youth academy in the south Indian state of Tamil Nadu, where Chennai is the main city, and soccer schools across the region. Finding the next Mohamed Salah in India is the goal, but developing a fanbase in India is an extra benefit.

# Diversification

As a business strategy, diversification may be considered one of the riskiest moves for a football club. However, we firmly believe it also holds the greatest potential for return on investment. Despite their widespread media attention and the enormous followers they have on social media, football clubs often experience limited financial gains. Companies in different industries may struggle to attract similar media attention or customer engagement levels but still achieve higher revenues. We contend that traditional revenue streams available to football clubs are too limited and that they should explore a more diverse range of options.

We recommend reviewing its cost structures if a football club is uncertain where to invest or what industries would suit its brand. One powerful move is to turn cost streams into revenue streams. For example, a football club could acquire a marketing agency and create a department dedicated to developing a new season ticket campaign. Using the club's relationships and media attention, the marketing agency can attract new clients and business opportunities to expand the football club's profits. The football club can pay for its marketing and content creation departments without incurring additional costs while increasing its expertise by utilising these profits.

This approach can be applied to other areas such as real estate (by reducing the cost of player accommodations), food and beverage services, pitch maintenance, IT solutions, training equipment, and medical goods. The aim of diversification is threefold: firstly, to lower costs for the club, thereby increasing profits and improving financial stability. Secondly, the club will attract a more diverse range of expertise within the organisation, which can result in better decision-making and problem-solving capabilities. Finally, if these companies develop and achieve significant revenues, they could become football club sponsors, reducing the risk of losing a sponsor during challenging economic times.

Football clubs are currently focusing on investing in players, which is not without risk. The transfer of players is a complex and unpredictable process, and poor performance, injuries, or lack of teamwork can result in significant losses. Even the most accomplished football players can struggle after being transferred to a new team, as illustrated by the experiences of Romelu Lukaku at Chelsea in 2021, Zlatan Ibrahimovic at Barcelona in 2009, and Philippe Coutinho at Barcelona in 2018. Spending over €100M on a player who fails to play regularly and is loaned back to their previous club one year later for a fee of €8M per season like in the case of Lukaku, is not uncommon. I contend that some of this money could be better invested in developing new revenue streams and lowering costs to create a healthier enterprise.

The City Football Group is one football entity that has adopted a diversification growth strategy. They have acquired multiple indoor 5-a-side pitches in the United States, which they run cost-efficiently. Approximately ten of these complexes generate a yearly profit of €10–15M, which covers many additional costs within the group.

## Key takeaways

- Few football clubs have long-term growth strategies and are stuck with short-term thinking.
- Owing to the uncertainty of sporting results, the lack of continuity in the football industry makes club managers afraid of taking risks and implementing growth strategies. They prefer to spend their financial resources on players who will nearly make the bench.
- Analyse the current club level (local, regional, domestic, international) and prepare strategic plans to grow to the next level.
- Dare to think outside the box and do not follow another club's path blindly.

# References

Beek, E. V. (2019). Global Football: Defining the rules of the changing game. In D. P. Simon Chadwick, *Routledge Handbook of Football Business and Management* (pp. 20–33). Taylor & Francis.

European Club Association. (2015). In K. S. Olivier Jarosz, *ECA Club Management Guide* (p. 80). ECA.

Pueckler, C. G. (2015). *The Internationalization Process of a Leading European Football Club*. Copenhagen Business School.

# 21 Corporate social responsibility

Simon Van Kerckhoven and
Martijn Ernest

Bas Schnater (Fan Engagement Consultant) and Geoff Wilson (Sports Strategy and Marketing Consultant) developed a conceptual framework for how football clubs, federations, and leagues can increase attendance on matchdays. Derived from the firm understanding that relying solely on results is a poor and unsustainable strategy to engage supporters in the long term, they designed the so-called GAM (Growing Attendance Model) (Geoff Wilson – Bas Schnater). The basic assumption of the GAM is that stakeholders in sports, specifically the football industry, should focus on the elements within their control (e.g. pricing, customer service, stadium cleanliness, and comfort) and mitigate against the elements which are not directly impressionable.

The GAM is broken into three broad elements: foundation necessities, resource commitment, and activities. Firstly, for a football organisation to broaden its fan base, a clearly defined vision, mission, and culture must be implemented. Progress can be made only when the organisation is aware that growing attendance should be, next to Sporting results, part of the long-term agenda. Aligning all the departments of the organisation and allocating the necessary resources to reach this goal is the first step in setting clear objectives. Second, human capital and economic resources should be efficiently used. Encouraging and engaging leadership forms the basis for committing resources responsibly. Establishing marketing research based upon analysing of all transactional data, upgrading customer service by improving front-line fan contact, and getting the right message to the right person at the right time by structuring the organisation's communication strategy, are key areas to invest in. Finally, the GAM focusses on implementing

DOI: 10.4324/9781003312680-24

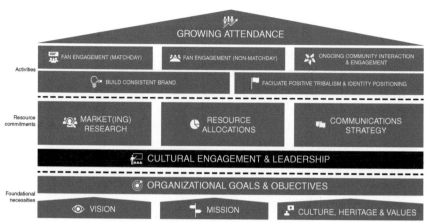

*Figure 21.1* Growing attendance model. (Used with permission GAM)
(Geoff Wilson & Bas Schnater, 2018.)

activities to realise its strategic elements. The next activities are key success factors in growing attendance sustainability by allowing and facilitating positive tribalism and identification: improved fan experience during match day, improved fan engagement activities, ongoing community interaction, consistent brand building, and activations regarding brand identification (Figure 21.1).

One of the key building blocks in this model is a club's focus on establishing ongoing interaction and engagement with its community. The community forms the basis and provides vital energy for a football entity. For professional football clubs, their active community of fans has been a source of revenue, support, and criticism ever since their creation. Numerous activations can be proposed to trigger active and passive supporters to interact with a football club, ranging from co-branding through sponsorship activation to using digital marketing tools and enhancing the matchday fan experience. This chapter describes the role of CSR and foundation or community trust activities as a tool for engaging with the community and growing attendance. The assumption is that the relationship between a club and its environment effectively represents the value of its cumulative social capital and is conditioned by actions and perceptions: on the one hand, actions generate results and affect perceptions, and on the other hand, in many cases, perceptions enable actions to take place.

# CSR strategy

Apart from the public-spirited and humanitarian obligations, football clubs must tackle social issues owing to their prominent societal role. CSR activities via a community trust or foundation can be a crucial step towards integration and success off the pitch. Well-structured and meaningful CSR activities can develop a more open and inclusive approach to community relations and engage more people in the club's operations. To find out how football clubs can leverage the work they are doing through a foundation or trust to benefit fan relationships, the GAM provides the framework for setting out a foundation' or community trust's strategy:

A. **Foundational necessities:** It all starts with the mission, vision, and goal-setting of the organisation. Selecting the right method of CSR implementation should be planned carefully following the overall culture and values of the organisation. The management team of the football club should, first, be thinking about how they want to assist the community; the motivation must be authentic and intrinsic before thinking about commercial gain. The club's identity plays a big role. Success can be booked only by setting out a clear, coherent alignment between the mission of the foundation or trust and the strategic plan of the football club.

B. **Resource commitments:** After deciding why the club should engage with the community by establishing a foundation or trust, the next step is to commit resources to the cause. Starting off with market research is the way to go. Questions to ask: 'What has the club done in the past in terms of charity work?', 'What are other clubs doing, and what is there to learn from them (benchmark)?', 'Is the league or federation supporting CSR?', 'Is the local, regional or federal government supporting projects where a CSR plan can be created around?', 'What is the overall geographical reach of the club and whom to target?', and 'What are the needs of the club's direct community?'. After obtaining a clear idea of the target group, resources must be brought to the table. In the start-up phase, reasonable investment is predominant. Knowing that 23% of the European Club Association member clubs allocated a budget between 10.000 EURO and 50.000 EUR0 on CSR programmes, it is not a big hurdle to invest in this section of club management (European Club Association, 2018). Finally, in this phase, the establishment of a clear communication strategy will ensure that the club can reach the right person at the right time with the right message. Over time this will contribute to establishing an ever-greater identification between the club and the community it is involved in.

C. **Activities:** When the strategic plan is formalised, budget and human resources are allocated, and the target groups are fixed, the foundation's or community trust's staff can implement and organise activities. These social activities are often only linked with standardised non-matchday activations, e.g. visiting a local school, assisting at a foodbank, bringing presents to hospitalised fans, and writing a cheque to a local charity. However, for CSR activities to have a positive impact on a club's brand and create an ongoing interaction with the community, clubs must take it further: focussing on raising employability in the region by opening a job fair, supporting educational projects by teaming up with local schools, entering international campaigns to ban racism from the stadium, and taking actions to promote environmentally responsible practices. These examples show that the foundations need to transcend traditional activities. Suppose matchday activations are consistently alternated with non-matchday community interactions. In that case, brand awareness will grow, and the brand's identity will be promoted as a force for good in the community.

Following the GAM to organise, optimise and activate a club's foundation or community trust, CSR and community management can be seen as a tool for relationship building with locals and, eventually, growing stadium attendance. Therefore, it would be naïve of a club to consider these community activities as only a way to 'give back'. Without minimalising the important social role that a football club has in an institutional context. Clubs also need to see the value CSR activities have towards further commercialisation. Approaching CSR and the development of a foundation as an investment rather than a cost can help the club raise its profile and positively impact partnership development through co-branding with non-football brands and raising government or European Union funding. It is important to remember that all the above suggestions can only be effective if they are executed on a long-term strategy. A one-off event will not assure fans or sponsors to engage with the football brand immediately; normally, a 40-week programme built around one specific topic should be the aim, year after year.

# Case studies

A. **Hamburg SV-Kids:** The ambassador for the Hamburg SV foundation is Dino Hermann. The name might sound familiar as he has an Instagram page with over 39.000 followers. The club turns the spotlight on its foundation through this social media page. In this way, sporting results become irrelevant to the communication of social activities, and the official mascot is very popular among the crowd. He has his performance show at the stadium during matchday, close access to the first team, and over 600 private events per season. He became so popular in the media that he had sponsors, which brought in extra revenues for the foundation.

B. **AIK Fotboll** – The Digital Locker Room: The Swedish football club AIK introduced an educational program focussed on young football players, team leaders, and parents to address the issue of harassment on social media and digital platforms. They demonstrated the possible effects of harassment and bullying and improved the management and safety of their online platforms and forums. The initiative was introduced through a nationwide campaign. In addition to the campaign, AIK followed up on the results of the campaign and worked to decrease the number of such events and incidental reports. For this initiative, they were nominated for the ECA Social Impact Awards 2022.

C. **Apollon Limassol FC** – Show Racism the Red Card: Just after the turn of the century, Apollon Limassol FC spotted racist abuse in and around their stadium. A serious problem that at that time occurred all over Cyprus. The club focussed on prevention by passing on the right message to young children to ban any form of racism from childhood by launching a nationwide campaign called Show Racism the Red Card. This shows that through football people from different backgrounds and countries can work together to achieve great results was the main objective. Informative school visits, campaigns at the stadium, and advertised announcements on all the club's official applications turned the campaign into a nationwide movement. Owing to the involvement of different public and political institutions, NGOs (Non-Governmental Organisations), and partners, the costs for Apollon Limassol FC were very limited. Similar campaigns are at this moment in place in the UK (the red card) and via the European Football for Development Network (show racism the red card).

**D. FC Inter Milano** – Inter Campus: Inter Campus contributes to the development of local communities worldwide, supporting educational, social, and sanitary protection programmes by local partners. Currently, Inter Campus has been active in 29 countries, employing 200 educators and serving nearly 10,000 children from 6 to 13 years of age. Each project is implemented via a structured process in seven phases: feasibility study and selection of local partners, official jersey delivery and technical clinics, setting up communication lines with local educators and volunteers, launching different educational activities, media promotion, monitoring, and site visits. For example, since 2000, Inter Campus has been committed contributing to Israel and Palestine, working with several organisations for peace on the two conflicting sides. This global initiative has proven its value to the overall brand recognition of Inter. Next, the club can collaborate with institutional (United Nations Development Program, United Nations Children's Fund and United Nations Office on Sport for Development and Peace) and commercial (Pirelli, TunisAir, Turkish Airlines, and Piccini Group) partners.

## Mistakes in CSR

Unfortunately, not all CSR projects or foundations are successful. Some projects never impact society, while others disappear in silence. The main reasons why CSR projects fail or have no impact on the community are:

1. Operations grow too quickly
2. Lack of accommodation or facilities
3. Internal assumptions over market research
4. Underestimation of the importance of co-production/collaborations
5. Giving away too much, to too many, too often (too much for free)
6. Work/life balance of employees

CSR does not mean that everything should be free. It means that the focus must be on the social aspect and not on making profits. The club creates a certain expectation from the ones they are targeting by giving away everything for free. We often see that CSR projects aim to create joyful activities. We mean, one-off events that are great for children and their parents. For sure, they all will have enjoyed the amazing day. *Unfortunately, the family will still have their issues and challenges for the other 364 days of the year.*

A better, more structured strategy can be set up in collaboration with the city council, to analyse the most common challenges in the local society and collaborate to solve those issues in a structured way. This can be achieved by organising language or economic classes at the stadium or organising a job fair for those who can barely afford food and beverages. We advise football clubs to look at their home city or town before implementing a regional or international strategy.

## Key takeaways

- CSR is the bridge between fans and the football club. It connects and unites different fan groups, players, employees, and boardroom members.
- It is a big factor in attracting more home game attendance and increasing the club's popularity.
- Focus first on social projects within the local community and only expand the region together with the growth of the club.
- CSR does not necessarily need to be a cost for the club. These organisations can often be self-sustainable through the support from other institutes such as the government or third parties.

## References

European Club Association. (2018). In O. Jarosz, *ECA Club Management Guide*. ECA.

Geoff Wilson – Bas Schnater. (2018). *Growing Attendance Model – GAM*.

# PART IV

# Conclusion

Reflections on the future of football club management

# 22 The evolution of football business

In this book's introduction, the question of why there have been so many fan protests against club owners or club directors recently and whether football clubs are being managed in the best possible way was asked. Contrary to prevailing sentiments that the football industry has peaked and is experiencing a decline in popularity, my professional assessment deems such statements as unfounded. Despite undergoing a turbulent period, the football industry continues to gain momentum and attract increasing numbers of enthusiasts. This is due to the innovative approach adopted by the football world, continually developing new assets like eSports and women's football. However, it is imperative to acknowledge that the governance of football needs to evolve towards a more transparent and ethical framework. Such changes would ensure that the football industry continues to flourish.

The eSports industry has seen tremendous growth in revenue, players, and spectators. As in every industry revenues will increase with more spectators or potential customers. However, what recently changed is that brands are investing heavily in eSports marketing, with major events and tournaments being organised. In addition to tournaments and online gaming, live streaming on Twitch significantly impact eSports and the entire gaming industry. However, also, YouTube has been a real catalysator for the industry reaching millions of fans with pre-recorded videos of how eSporters are gaming.

Like in any other industry, COVID-19 greatly impacted eSports and changed its entire nature. Owing to the pandemic, spectators spiked across all live-streaming platforms as people were obliged to spend time at home during the lockdown. Nevertheless, all professional live tournaments and events were cancelled, which slowed down the growth during this time. In 2019 there were approximately 200 million occasional viewers and

DOI: 10.4324/9781003312680-26

197 million eSports enthusiasts, according to Newzoo, with a yearly increase of approximately 12.3%. Newzoo predicts that by 2024, the number of occasional viewers will have grown to 291.6 million and that there will be approximately 285.7 million eSports enthusiasts. The biggest growth is expected in new markets such as the Middle East, Africa, Asia-Pacific, and Latin America. However, also, countries like India and Brazil are on the rise (Newzoo, 2022).

The total eSports revenue in 2019 was approximately €957 million, according to Newzoo. Owing to the pandemic, revenue growth has not only been slowed down but decreased. Despite this decrease, the estimations for revenues in 2024 are approximately 1.617 million euros, which would mean a yearly growth of 11.1%. The main part of these revenues is expected to come from China.

Newzoo estimated that the total eSports revenues in 2018 were made up as follows (Figure 22.1).

eSports is still very dependent on sponsorship revenues, but ticketing and media rights are expected to boom within the coming years (Geyser, 2022).

However, what is the link between eSports and football? It started with football players playing a popular; game FIFA (now EA Sports FC) and started streaming some of their games, and fans loved it. After that, it developed fast as football clubs started recruiting eSports players to play alongside FIFA's other strategy and shooting games, such as Counterstrike or League of Legends. One of the reasons why football clubs have been developing their eSports department has to do with the decline in stadium attendance and the decrease in annual growth. Football clubs hope to reach the younger generation and make them become a fan of their football club by tapping into the eSports hype.

This strategy and logical reasoning for the bigger football clubs such as Real Madrid, Olympique Lyon, Manchester City FC, and FC Barcelona is

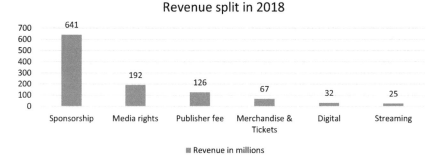

*Figure 22.1* Split of revenue streams in eSports (see Newzoo, 2022)

fully understood, but not for smaller teams who are not yet at that level. Smaller football clubs still have so many other priority issues that need to be addressed rather than focussing on the creation of new assets with an uncertain outcome and no direct large revenue stream nor any fan engagement with direct impact.

Nevertheless, some football clubs have taken their eSports strategy to the next level by partnering with professional eSports organisations. AS Roma announced in 2017 their new joint venture with Fnatic to build a strong legacy in eSports and engage with current and new fans.

One of the early adopters of eSports was Besiktas. In 2015 they acquired the Aces High team and renamed it 'Besiktas eSports'. In 2020 Olympique Lyonnais partnered with the technology company LDLC Group, the parent company of Team LDLC that rebranded to 'LDLC OL'. They seek to develop the eSports ecosystem in the greater Lyonnais region, emphasising youth, associations, companies, and communities to attract native and international talent. They also seek to construct a 16.000-seater arena near the football stadium of Olympique Lyonnais, which will host major international eSports competitions.

There is little doubt that with such a fast-growing industry, eSports tournament prize money and players' earnings are also increasing rapidly. In 2019, the total global prize money for a total of 5.591 eSports tournaments was €236 million, so the mean tournament prize pool was €42.000. With 28.336 active players at these tournaments, the mean earnings were €8.400 per player. However, according to eSports Earnings, the prize money recorded has increased to €1.3 billion. With prize money over €2 million for the Rocket League Championship Series 2021–2022 – World Championship where Team BDS won 600.000 Euro (eSports Earnings, 2022).

Therefore, if football clubs developed a strong marketing and revenue strategy in eSports, we all would favour these developments. However, that does not mean that every football club or league is ready to enter the amazing world of eSports.

In addition to eSports, we all have seen the development of another fantastic asset in football in the past decade, Women's football. Finally! Record after records are being broken. Attendances are increasing, and the media is showing more and more interest in the sport. Women's football is by far more popular than ever before. The UEFA European Championship, held in the UK and won by England's women defeating Germany 2–1 in extra time, was the highlight of summer 2022, With 87,192 fans in Wembley witnessing the Lionesses bring the cup home.

However, this was only the third highest attendance in 2022, with 91,553 attendances watching Barcelona at Camp Nou face the rivals of Real Madrid in the quarterfinals of the Women's Champions League and an even bigger crowd of 91,648 people turning up to watch Barcelona beating Wolfsburg 5–1 in the semi-finals of the Women's Champions League. These numbers show the potential that women's football has and that its popularity is increasing yearly.

Despite these excellent results in the top games at the UEFA European Championship and the UEFA Champions League, the numbers for a league game in Belgium or any other smaller country cannot be matched. However, even in these smaller countries, there has been an increased popularity and fan attendance. In Belgium, the Belgian Red Flames broke in September 2022 their record from 2018 in the qualifying match against Norway by selling out the stadium of OH-Leuven, 8,765 fans! Not only are the federations investing in the development of women's football, but broadcasters such as Eleven Sports (now part of DAZN) and Sky Sports have also made huge investments. The Football Association announced before the UEFA Championship a record-breaking three-year deal with Sky Sports and the BBC for the broadcast rights of the Women's Super League; A deal worth around £8 million a year and the biggest broadcast deal of any professional women's football league in the world.

One of the main issues in women's football is the salaries of players. Lucy Bronze, one of the national team players of England who won the UEFA European Championship, was fortunate in signing sponsorship deals with Nike and Visa, and each England player received a bonus of £55.000 for winning the UEFA European Championship.

Unfortunately, many female football players still play for a full-time salary of £21.000 per year. Much less compared to what male Premier League players are earning in a week. Despite all the positive efforts over the past years, the economic setting is still very different from the men's game and cannot yet be compared to each other. The male Premier League brings approximately £10 billion for domestic and international rights in the next three years. The commercial rights have also grown to £430 million. That is approximately £3.5 billion per year, while the English Women's Super League record broadcasting contract holds a value of £8 million per year. A comprehensive research report from FIFA on women's football found that 70% of women's football clubs internationally operate at a loss. Just 13% of women's clubs generate revenues over €1 million; more than half of those revenues come from sponsorship deals (FIFA, 2022).

One of the reasons could be that women's football is modelled around men's football, with many women's teams being affiliated with men's football clubs. While this holds many benefits, such as sharing facilities and infrastructure, a ready-made supporter base, and the human resources of the men's team, there are also some downsides. The long-term future of women's football is dependent on the men's team might hold the commercial growth of women's football back.

In the USA, the most developed women's football market, half of the football teams have no affiliation with the men's team. Therefore, there is a greater focus on providing better quality, higher capacity stadia, better marketing, and communication while having high match attendances. Research has also shown that negotiating broadcast rights exclusively for women's teams generates seven times more revenue from broadcasting than leagues that negotiate rights alongside their men's competition. According to FIFA's research, this also counts for the negotiation of sponsorship contracts. When negotiating sponsorship contracts exclusively for their women's team, they generate twice as much in revenue.

On the governance level, there is also an ongoing debate concerning financial distribution. Money flows to the more successful clubs, which creates a selected number of top teams. This causes a competitive balance problem, where a few clubs are so much stronger, and the rest cannot even hope to compete. This means that the winner of the league or a tournament is very predictable from the start, making the matches less exciting. Competitive balance has become an issue in the men's game for years, making top competitions such as the Champions League very predictable. Competitive balance is something women's football should keep in mind in its further development.

The conclusion is that there is still a lot of work to create a more sustainable environment despite the absolute economic growth in football for the last decades. Our beloved game has been globalised and monetised. Think about on-demand streaming, commercialising match highlights on social media, documentaries on Netflix, podcasts, NFTs, fan tokens, and online fantasy games such as Sorare. Total club revenues have grown by millions, yet many of the biggest brands in football still have huge debts, and some are struggling year after year to be break-even. However, how much further can commercial activities be developed and new assets or revenue streams created? Is it not time to start rebuilding that deeper connection with fans, creating a long-term sustainable vision, and being consistent towards the brand identity?

Unfortunately, there have been too many scandals damaging the reputation of football. Money laundering, bribery, match-fixing, and tax fraud have all been linked with recent scandals in the global football industry. There is still much work to do to clear football of corruption. The recent implementations and changes around governance principles, clearinghouses, and the development of educational courses have been a big improvement, making the industry more transparent and ethical, but we are not there yet.

After analysing some of the most recent scandals, one consistent issue is the decision power one person holds at a club or federation. Is this something that can be avoided? Maybe not. However, the evolution of fans asking for more transparency, insights, and a bigger voice at the decision table is something to keep in mind to avoid power control by one person at a football club. Some football clubs have chosen a certain power distribution to leave no room for corruption. Fan groups holding an X-percentage of club shares and several seats in the boardroom, the creation of a 'golden share' for the non-profit organisation of the club to safeguard the vision, club colours, and other club assets, socios having voting rights to elect their club president or the famous 50 + 1 rule in Germany. However, those adjustments have not always been as effective as expected, and some of the clubs with those implementations still experienced difficult times owing to mismanagement, greed, or corruption.

Is there a perfect solution? Maybe not. Nevertheless, with all the technology and global connectivity we have available today, would it not be great to connect global fans of a football club and involve them in the overall club strategies, not just by asking their opinion through surveys but by really working with them as if they were boardroom members. To reinvent a club's membership or the privileges of socios and to design a new system where fans have more control over the decisions being taken in the boardroom? Looking back at the introduction of this book, where I referred to fan protest and unsustainable club management situations, I believe that such involvement of fans on a strategic level can prevent fan protests and create a more transparent industry. This might build that deeper, closer connection between fans and club management, and who knows, it might

210

even bring financial sustainability to the clubs. Because the last thing fans want to do is take any big risks that could lead to the bankruptcy of their beloved football club.

# References

eSports Earnings. (2022). Retrieved from Esports Earnings: https://www.esportsearnings.com/

FIFA. (2022). *Setting the Pace – FIFA Benchmarking Report Women's Football*. FIFA.

Geyser, W. (2022, August 1). *The Incredible Growth of eSports*. Retrieved from Influencer Marketing Hub: https://influencermarketinghub.com/esports-stats/

Newzoo. (2022). *Global eSports & Live Streaming Market Report*. Newzoo.

# Index